Table of Contents

How to Teach Preschool Ballet

A Guidebook for Teachers

Gina Mayer

Mayer Arts, Inc.

How to Teach Preschool Ballet

A Guidebook for Teachers

by
Gina Mayer

First publication: January 2012
Revised: January 2020

ISBN-13: 978-1500631567
ISBN-10: 1500631566

Published by Mayer Arts, Inc.
Cover designed by Gina Mayer

www.wish-upon-a-ballet.com

For my graceful and creative Juliana, who teaches me new things everyday.

Introduction

Teaching preschool dance, or any kind of teaching for that matter, is an art. I remember the first time I heard the phrase "teaching artist" when I was living in New York years ago. That phrase made such an impact on me. It made me feel I am not just a dancer with a teaching job but someone who is dedicated to learning and perfecting the art of teaching the performing arts. The performing arts are very important to me and being able to pass that love on to someone else in the most effective way possible is a wonderful opportunity. Therefore teaching is not just a job it is an art. Hopefully you are interested in reading this book because it is important to you as well! And you understand it is something that has to be learned and developed with care over time.

It frustrates me when I hear the phrase, Those who can't - teach." What an untrue statement. If you can't dance, sing, paint, act, etc. you shouldn't be teaching those disciplines to other people. I am in no way a "Prima Ballerina". However I love ballet and have studied ballet technique most of my life. What I am most proud of is I am able to effectively communicate technique, have a controlled class, inspire my students and create good dancers. That is something not everybody can do. This is the art.

Why write a book dedicated to the art of teaching dance to preschoolers? What is so different about preschoolers? Preschoolers are not going to be learning pirouettes and fouettés so it can't be that hard right? No, you are not teaching pirouettes, but teaching preschoolers to be in a class, follow the teacher and actually learn steps and choreography is a different kind of challenge.

First of all, I have been an instructor of the performing arts and a business owner for a very long time and have hired many teachers. What I have found is there is definitely a lack of training for performing arts instructors specifically for younger ages. Most new instructors have recently come out of a studio or college dance program and are used to being with students their own age who can handle complex choreography and technique. Dance education majors have mostly received training for students in the K-12 school system. Teaching preschool students was not their focus. I have also come across dance studios that don't know how to create a successful preschool program. Many little ones want to leap and spin and be in a ballet class. The market is huge! A studio should have a solid preschool program that can be a base for the rest of their school.

The second point is, those who "can", meaning those who have professional careers as artists, can't all teach. You may have taken a class from someone famous or that has a well known reputation in the dance world. Many studios, colleges and professional dance schools bring in master teachers. I have taken many dance classes from instructors with impressive professional careers. Some are very committed to passing on their knowledge and experiences while others just run a class and hope their reputation gets them through.

So how do you teach preschoolers ballet? Preschoolers can handle choreography and a little technique but it has to be approached differently. Preschoolers are a completely different group of learners. They need high energy and tons of creativity. We can't create the same class for them as we do for older students.

Let's talk a moment about technique in respect to preschoolers. You can't just say, "point your toes". Well you can, but it is not the most effective way to teach a step. How do you really communicate what you want? For a preschooler it is not fun to be told to simply point their toes time after time. You need to make it creative. Maybe they can they pretend to dip their toes in a pond like Sleeping Beauty? For older students that can grasp technique the subject becomes much more complicated. The "toes" are really the whole foot or a continuation of the whole leg which is not just pointing it is stretching from the center. So first, you need to know your technique and know your audience. Don't try to force technique on preschoolers. You will lose them. For preschoolers, technique needs to be fun.

Teaching someone to dance is not easy. You can show someone how you do a particular movement, but how do you teach someone to have their body do what your body can do? You need to learn to communicate like a teacher. You can use words, you can actually move the students' bodies to where you want them to be and you can demonstrate. Really good teachers are able to see what each individual student needs and teach them in a way that helps them learn and grow.

My name is Gina Mayer and I have been teaching preschool ballet since 1996. My students call me, "Ms. Gina Ballerina"! I love preschoolers. They can be the most fun to teach. Nobody just wants to have fun more than a preschooler. They twirl and spin like they are ready for the American Ballet Theatre. They leap around the floor with the utmost enthusiasm. Their smiles are infectious and their giggles are contagious. However, they can also not listen to a word you say. They can be more interested in an ant crawling on the floor than a tendu. If you are not sure how to teach them, they can be frustrating to a point that makes you want to cry.

I remember very well the first year I taught preschool dance. I was employed by a company that taught tap, jazz, ballet, and creative movement to preschoolers in preschools. I traveled from preschool to preschool teaching children in the Minneapolis and St. Paul metro area. Some classes were very easy and I would have a lot of fun. In other classes I would pull my hair out trying to encourage the children to listen. I did actually break down and cry in one class. No matter what I did it seemed the children would not listen. It is interesting to look back at it now. I remember being upset but I don't remember how I taught the class. It would have been nice to have my present self at that class to help out my past self. I know I have changed very much as a teacher over the years and would be able to have a much different experience today.

The interesting thing is I continue to change. I think I have been very successful as a teacher throughout my career. Even though I was not the most trained teacher when I first started, I still had a passion for teaching. I loved children and dance and wanted to pass my love of dance to my students. This was a good start. You need to have those attributes if you are going to be a good teacher. Now however, I know the preschooler. I know what makes them tick, so to speak. I usually know what they are going to do before they do it. I know how they are going to respond in different situations. I know what they like and don't like. This comes from experience.

Now, I am going to pass that experience on to you. If you are reading this you also have a passion for teaching young students and want to be the best you can. Good for you! Your students deserve to have a great experience. We want them to learn and have fun. This is a gift you can give these children that they will remember for the rest of their lives. Most of my memories of being three are from my first dance class. Not only can you create wonderful memories for your students but you may create future ballet dancers and appreciators. We need to keep the art of ballet and other arts alive. We can do that with great teachers. You have a responsibility to your students and the arts!

Since writing the first edition of this book a few positive things have changed for me as an instructor. The first change is I am even more comfortable teaching preschool ballet. I always wondered if I would enjoy teaching preschoolers after 20 plus years and now I can say I definitely do! My students still bring me joy every class. Maybe more so now because I am even more comfortable with them. I completely trust that I am in control so I can relax and have fun! There have been many more students that have come through my door I have learned from. Even though most preschoolers are very alike in what they enjoy and how they behave there is always going to be someone with a new personality I have never experienced before. Someone new I get to meet. Each child adds to my inner library of experience.

Another change is the internet and social media have exploded. There are so many resources for teachers to share experiences and gain knowledge. That is great! But what I have discovered more than all the opportunities to learn online are the online communities for teachers to share their experiences. I have learned how many passionate teachers are out there. They are continuously sharing what they love about their students and what they love about dance. They are reaching out for support and supporting others. They put their hearts into their businesses no matter what. I have truly been inspired by all of you and I am glad to be a part of this wonderful community!

The last amazing change I would like to mention is we are now more sensitive than ever to each other's diverse needs. Issues are being brought up in the world, and specifically in the dance world, about how people should be treated. One example is there are now ballet shoes to match different skin tones. Another is men are opening up about how their love of dance didn't stop them even if they were bullied for dancing growing up. We don't all have to fit in one bubble. There are so many of us with unique gifts to share. This is something I will address more in chapter seven.

There are endless benefits of dance for people of all ages. This is especially true for preschoolers. Preschoolers will learn how to behave in a class setting, how to express themselves creatively, become more confident, strengthen their coordination and build their minds. We, as teachers, have the wonderful opportunity to start their love of dance off on the right foot!

Thank you for coming on this journey with me to explore the world of teaching preschool ballet. A world I love and take very seriously. Follow this guidebook and you will have a fun and smooth preschool class. The comments I receive from parents are that their children have so much fun in my classes and they can't believe how much their children learn. They also can't believe I can have a full class of three and four year olds follow me and do exactly what I say. If you follow this guidebook you will have the same success! Remember "Those who can - TEACH!"

Chapter 1

Before You Even Enter a Classroom ~ Preparation

There is much to be done before you even enter a preschool dance class. What are your goals for your class? What are you going to teach? How are you going to teach the material? How are you going to present yourself? These are all elements you need to consider before teaching a class. Let's go through exactly what you will have to do before your class begins.

What Are Your Goals?

After you have decided you would like to teach dance, you need to have clear goals for yourself, your class and your students. Here are the goals I have when I go into a dance class.

There are a few objectives I keep in mind for myself as a

teacher. The most fundamental one is, I constantly try to be present when I prepare for classes and when I am teaching my classes. This way, I can monitor how I am doing and how I can improve. How can I be a better teacher today than I was yesterday? Taking good care of myself is another goal. I want to feel good when I am teaching. It is fun to be able to keep up with my students and dance and leap around with plenty of energy. Finally, another one of my goals is to have fun! Being fortunate enough to be able to enjoy your career is a gift. I know if I am having fun the students are having fun.

For my classes, I have specific goals as well. When I am planning my classes, I want my curriculum to be fun and engaging. I choose material I think the students will love and will help me teach the material I want to teach. Another goal is I want my curriculum to be original and new. There is always a new dance or activity to share with my classes.

Most importantly, I have goals for my students. The first goal is, I want my students to have fun. The second goal is, I want my students to learn. Lastly, I want my students to feel good about themselves in my class. It is not only important to have them learn and have fun but I want to increase their confidence and self-esteem as well.

The intentions you have for your classes are very important. If you go into a class without knowing what you want to accomplish, the class will reflect that. If you have a clear direction for your class, you will not fail in carrying it out. Your intentions will always be present in your mind.

Being Professional

Let's talk about how to be professional when you are a dance teacher. In fact, we must be professional in any job. But what exactly does that mean?

When you think about being professional, first think about

your demeanor. How do you come across to others? Are you upbeat and happy? Do you appear confident? If you feel good that's great! If you don't feel good you will need to figure out why and change your attitude. If you have a cold or didn't sleep well the night before you will need to put that aside for the sake of your class. This way, you will come across as more professional.

How you appear is another factor in being professional. What is the proper attire for a dance teacher? This depends on where you teach and what discipline you teach. You will need to ask the director of the studio, at which you are teaching, what they prefer. If you are working on your own, it will be up to you. For pre-ballet teachers a leotard, tights, skirt and ballet shoes are the most appropriate. If you are more comfortable in other dance attire, be sure to ask your program director if it is alright to wear an alternative outfit. You could wear leggings and a t-shirt or tank top if that is acceptable. You do want to be comfortable, however just make sure you still look like a dancer.

Be sure you are taking good care of yourself. Get enough rest before class days. Eat well and exercise. Taking class for yourself is a great way to keep in shape while enjoying what you love! We are in a business that uses our bodies. Being healthy is important.

Being well organized is another way to be professional. Always be early to class to give yourself plenty of time to get ready. Have any information ready to communicate to your families they might need. This might be information about days off, upcoming performances or information about an individual student's progress.

Lastly, know your material and follow the rest of the guidelines in this book. If you do, your students, their parents and your studio directors will be impressed!

Curriculum ~ What Are You Going to Teach?

Before you can teach a good ballet class, you need to have a well thought out and creative curriculum. How you come up with your curriculum may depend on where you teach and whether your program director provides you with your curriculum. In all cases you will be teaching a few basic ballet steps and presenting them in a creative way.

I provide my teachers with the curriculum, because I have created a preschool ballet program I believe in. Places at which you teach will either have a curriculum, or they will expect you to come up with your own. The curriculum for your class may also depend on the kind of school at which you are teaching. A program may want a traditional ballet class or they may want a class that is freer to let the children explore.

I personally believe a class that has many creative games and activities will be more productive for preschoolers than a class that has the children repeating steps over and over and/or standing at the barre. Preschoolers learn best through creativity and imagination. The bottom line is, children will follow you in whatever you do if they can also play games and pretend to be their favorite characters. They truly learn better this way.

A parent may believe their four year old is too gifted to be with other preschoolers and would prefer them to be in an older class. This happens with older age groups as well. Parents, of course, want their children to be successful and grow. The only problem is, a child may be ready physically to move up to the next level, but emotionally they are not. Preschoolers learn through creativity. School age children also love to be creative but are ready to handle more technique. Preschoolers may be able to learn a bit of technique, but even then they may have a hard time remembering what you have told them. If you push a preschooler to be with older children they will most likely feel lost and overwhelmed. Let the little ones be little ones!

Come up with a child friendly theme and find songs that go with that theme. Think of some creative movement games as well. Preschoolers need to be able to imagine different situations, places, people or animals. Each song should have a story. Who are you singing and dancing about? Let's take an example of "Twinkle Twinkle Little Star". There are many different versions of this song that would go well with a ballet class. How can we spark the students imaginations? It is a song they know, which is helpful, and it has a pretty melody. Ask the students to pretend to look up at the night sky. Can they see stars? What do they look like? Can they wish on a star? What would they wish for? Can they be a star? If a star could dance, how would it dance? We could have a whole class on this one theme. Throw in some pliés and tendus and you will be all set!

Make sure you not only have enough material at each class but have extra songs and activities in case you need them. Be over prepared. You may need to change what you are teaching if something you planned is not working. Sometimes one dance will work with one group but not another. If a class looks bored you may need to move on. Some classes move through material faster than others. You may perform three activities in one class and five or six in another. There will be times when you finish all your material and you may have time to play some creative games or play with props. Have some creative movement games ready to go if there is time. Having extra games may also be helpful if the class is on the younger side or having a "squiggly" day and just can't focus very well on what you have prepared. The same is true with props. A parachute is great to have in class for a change of pace.

What ballet steps can preschoolers handle? There are a few basic ballet steps I make sure I cover each session. These include first position, second position, plié, relevé, and tendu. Usually I include arabesque and passé as well for fun and to practice balance. At the end of each session these are the steps I want my students to know and be able to show their families without my help. I will add trickier steps to mix it up from time to time but these are the ones I make sure to cover.

Please note there is a difference between relevé and elevé and also passé and retiré. At the preschool level however, trying to explain the difference is too much information. Giving too many facts interferes with our goal of keeping the class creative and light. Wait until students show a true passion for ballet to dive into such details.

Keep reading ahead for more information on how to teach ballet steps and how to run your class. There will be more specific examples about how a class should be handled from start to finish.

Know the Material ~ Ballet Technique

If you teach ballet it seems obvious that you should know how to dance ballet. This is true for any teacher of any discipline. You don't have to be a perfect dancer but you do need to have knowledge of what you are teaching, otherwise your students will pay the price.

Example:

I took my daughter to a gymnastics class with a program that offers gymnastics and dance to children. During my daughter's gymnastics class I could see the dance class through the window in another room. The students were taught ballet and tap. However the teacher did not appear to have dance experience. Yes, the children are three and four years old, but does that mean we shouldn't teach them real ballet?

I believe, as a teacher, you are responsible for knowing the subject you are teaching. This seems obvious but unfortunately I have witnessed dance teachers who do not seem to have proper technique or who do not use proper terms for steps. If you would like to teach ballet, then learn about it. If you have not studied dance in your past, then do it now. Not only take class, but read about ballet. I have to be honest, part of why I created wish-upon-a-ballet.com was for my own benefit. I wanted to learn more about ballet history, famous dancers etc. In addition, many parents of my students ask me ballet questions and I want to be knowledgeable.

Teachers should also keep training and taking classes. There are always new discoveries to be made when learning ballet. Continuing your training keeps you on top of your technique, sets a good example for your students and gives new ideas on how to teach. We are all still learning.

A three year old is not going to have any idea what your ballet training is and their parents may not as well, but that doesn't matter. Be respectful of the art of ballet and of your students. Know ballet.

Know the Material ~ Your Curriculum

It is much easier to teach a class when you know the dances and the steps you are going to be teaching by memory. I am not saying you can't have notes to look at from time to time. That is actually a good idea. I may have notes reminding me about my class order or any new choreography. But if you need to carry notes around with you and look at them often, that is a problem. You don't want to take too much time away from your class. Preschool students have very short attention spans and if you don't keep class moving they will find something else to do.

When a subject is new, you will have to practice at home until you can perform your dances without looking at your notes. Why is this important? In order to teach a preschool ballet class you need to be fully present. There are so many things you will have to focus on during your class. Are the children paying attention and following you? Do they understand the material? Are they having fun?

The dances need to be second nature in order for you to dance and give directions at the same time. For example, while you are dancing you may have to remind Susie to use her listening ears. Or, you could sing along with the songs to make the dances more fun for the children. Finally, you could remind the students what is coming up next so they don't fall behind. All this and dance at the same time.

If you do not know the material, the energy of your class may decrease and your students may find other things to do. Your class will run much smoother if you know your material by heart.

Find Your Teaching Style

I have watched many dance teachers in my career. When I watch them, I always notice their style of teaching. I have seen a range of styles, and to me, they all seem to fit between two categories. I call it the "Parent" style verses the "Big Kid" style. I teach with more of a mom like demeanor. I'm calm and nurturing but I still have a lot of energy and can be silly too! There are other teachers who act just like big, silly kids. There is no wrong way of teaching. Your personality will decide what your style is. Don't try to be something you are not.

Example:

I taught theater at a summer camp several years ago. During the summer I had a review with my supervisor. He commented on the fact that my style was very different than his. When he taught, he acted like a big goofball which the students loved. However, in my review he remarked that I had more of a calm energy when I taught. He seemed confused because he knew that the students had a great connection with me and had fun in my classes. He seemed to believe that there was only one way to teach children, when in fact there are many ways.

For me personally, the big kid style is fake. It is not natural and does not fit with my personality. I knew our styles were not the same and I knew there was nothing wrong with that. You don't need to be a goofball to be a good teacher. But if that is you, go for it!

Your style of teaching doesn't matter. What does matter is whether or not the children are having fun and paying attention in your class.

To sum up, it is so important to be prepared for your classes. You, as the teacher, are responsible for creating a class that is fun, engaging and actually teaches ballet! You can't just go to class and believe whatever happens, happens. You must put a lot of thought into the class as far as what you are going to teach and how you are going to teach it. Being prepared will help keep your students happy. It will benefit you as well because you will be much more relaxed and actually have fun too! Let's continue this idea into the classroom.

Chapter 1 "Pointes" to Remember

* Know Your Goals
* Be Professional
* Decide What You Are Going to Teach
* Know Your Technique
* Learn Your Curriculum
* Find Your Teaching Style

Chapter 2

In the Classroom Before Class Begins

Your preparation and professionalism are very important before you start your class. Before class is when your students and their parents see you for the first time. This is when they will create a first impression of you and what your class may be like. In this section, you will learn how to set the tone for your class in a positive way so everyone will be excited to take your class!

Be On Time

Always be on time for your class. Not only should you be on time, but everything should be ready to go at least five minutes before your class begins. I actually try for 10 minutes when I teach. There is a lot of planning to be done in order for you to be at your class on time. You need to decide how much time you need to make sure you are ready to go at the beginning of your class.

Here are some things you should think about before you are ready to start class:

* Do you need to pass out any notes to the parents?
* Is your music ready to go?
* Are your props easily accessible?
* Are you dressed? Shoes on? Hair out of your face?
* Do you need to go over any material?
* Do you know what you are going to cover that day?

Make sure you plan ahead for travel time. Living in Minnesota, my teachers and I deal with all kinds of road issues. The winter months are especially tricky and snowy days can really hold you up. Being in a large city we often deal with traffic and construction as well. Check all the elements before you leave for a class in order for you to arrive with plenty of time to prepare.

By being on time and ready to go with time to spare, you will have more time to relax before class. You will also have more time to chat with your students and their families and make strong connections with them. This will create trust with your customers. When your students and parents trust you, they will be more likely to enjoy your class and come back for more!

Be Happy!

We all have days we would rather just stay in bed under the covers. However, when you are teaching a class of little people, you must leave all your troubles behind you. This is true for any job.

Once you are in the parking lot of the dance studio or venue, you must turn on your happy teacher face. It is very easy to go to class when you feel good. How about when you are having a bad day? Do you tell the students and parents you are having a bad day? Do you tell them your car broke down or your significant other is being a jerk? No! Of course if you have developed a personal relationship with a parent or two, sharing certain information with them is not harmful. But be selective. I still don't believe sharing personal information with people that are your customers is a good idea. You probably can get away with talking about your car, but leave your partner out of any conversations.

If you are having a bad day, you must leave it in the car, bus, train or whatever mode of transportation took you to your class. When I leave my car I am immediately "Ms. Gina Ballerina". The feelings I may feel from any unfortunate situation in my life stays in my car. It will wait for me in the car when class is over. I see many of my students in the parking lot and nobody wants to hear about any issue I may be having. They just want to have a great dance class! Most of the time my students cheer me up anyway, and whatever was bothering me no longer bothers me by the time class is over. Be happy, positive and upbeat whenever you are in the presence of your students and their families.

Why is this important? It is important because you want to give the best class you can. If you come into class with a down attitude, the parents and children will worry that class won't be as good as it should be. They just want to have fun. You owe them that experience.

Example:

I went to view a class and the teacher came in and proceeded to prepare for class. I said "Hi!" very cheerfully and I asked her how she was. I expected her to just say "I'm good. How are you?" She however, was not having a good day and proceeded to tell me about it even as families were arriving. She didn't seem to realize her attitude would affect the quality of her class.

This teacher's class was not as fun or exciting as it should have been. I would have been happy to listen to her once her class was over and the students had left. However, the teacher should have left her problems in the car for the sake of her students. If you remember to do that, it will pay off. It will not only be good for your students, but it will be good for you and your career as a dance teacher.

Greet Your Students

This goes with the point above. Always notice your students and their parents when they arrive to class. Think about them as your guests. When someone comes in, welcome them and ask them how their day is going.

What happens if you just ignore your students when you first see them? How do you think that will affect your class?

Example:

At the same class I mentioned above the teacher, because she was too involved with her own issues, did not acknowledge anyone as they came into her room. She proceeded to prepare for her class and didn't look up at all. The parents dropped off their children, and left them in the room without saying anything to the teacher. This teacher did have a difficult time with the children's listening ears and I know this was part of the reason.

As a parent, it would be unacceptable for me to leave my child in a class where the teacher did not acknowledge me or my child when we came in the room. I would want to know the teacher saw my child so I could feel confident they would be well taken care of. Parents need to feel they are passing their children on to another responsible adult who is paying attention. If this is the first day of class make sure to introduce yourself. You may have to remind students and parents of your name often, in fact. It is very easy to forget someone's name especially if you are three. Everyone will be excited to know you as well as what your class is all about.

In addition, greeting someone when you see them is just the right thing to do. It makes people feel good when you notice them. It will also continue to build trust between you and your families. Then class will be off to a more positive start. The more positive you make your class at each opportunity the better the class will be.

If parents are bringing the students into class too early and you are still preparing for class, let them know. Still greet them with a smile, ask how everyone is doing but simply say you are not quite ready for the students and need a few more minutes. You can tell them you will let the students into the room five minutes before class. You can also have a policy that the door for the dance area does not open until five minutes before class. On the welcome letters I pass out to parents, it asks parents to please be respectful of their teacher's preparation time. Your time outside of class does need to be valued.

Even if you are trying to prepare for class, never ignore your customers. Always be polite and greet them. They are coming into your space and need to feel welcome.

Show Interest in Your Students

Not only should you greet your students and their parents, but be genuinely interested in them. Everyone will appreciate it if you are excited to see the children and are interested in their lives.

Try to remember something special the child, or the parent, sibling etc. has told you before. For example, "I remember you had a birthday last week! How was the party?" or "How was your vacation? It is so nice to have you all back!" People like it when you show interest in them.

Remember you are not just selling a ballet class you are selling yourself. Again, parents will be more likely to sign their children up for your class if they like you, not just what you teach. I will talk more about selling your class later on in this book. Of course however, always be real and sincere!

Communication With Parents

Communication is an important part of any relationship. Parents want to feel they are leaving their children in good hands. They want and need to feel you are a trustworthy person and their children are learning. They are leaving their precious babies with you. It is key the parents know you can be trusted. How do you do this?

There are a few ways to earn the parents' trust. Following the few rules I have already covered is a good start. Be happy as soon as you leave the car and say hello to parents and students when you see them. This will make everyone relax and feel at ease around you. Being professional by looking refreshed and being on time is key as well.

The other step you can take to make parents feel relaxed about leaving their children with you, is to constantly be in communication with them. Tell the parents what you are going to cover in class. If this is the first day of class, you can tell parents what you will be covering that day and over the entire session. You can also tell them what the students should learn by the end of the session. This will let the parents know you are prepared and actually have a plan for their children. If the parents like you and trust you, their children will have more fun. Not only that, but they will be more likely to sign their child up for class again.

If you have open classes the parents can more easily see what you are doing in class. If you have closed classes or if some parents drop their children off and pick them up after class, they don't always see what their children are doing. Even if parents can witness what you are doing in class they will still need the material to be explained to them. In all cases, it is a good idea to talk to the parents after class is over and the parents are picking up their children. Talk to everyone about what happened in class. For example, "Today we started learning 'Twinkle Twinkle little Star'. The children had such a good time! They learned first position and how to plié. Who can show their parents how to plié? Wow that's great!"

Another helpful idea for your classes is to make a handout that contains the dances, games and steps you will be focusing on. This can cover each day or the whole session. This way, parents can read about what you will be covering and take it home with them. Then, at home they can talk to their children about what they are doing in class. You can also post highlights of your curriculum on the door or a board so they can read about what you are doing as they pick up their children.

Parents want to know what their children are doing and what they are learning especially since it may be difficult for a preschooler to remember everything. It is important to them. Many parents want to feel their children are being educated as well as having fun. By being in constant communication with the parents they will know you are accomplishing both of those points and you have a good quality class.

Own Your Dance Space

When you are teaching a preschool dance class, or any class, you are in charge of the space. Think of it as your home. This means the space must be managed correctly as well as respected. How do you do that?

I like to think of myself as the mom of the space. I actually visualize I have long stretchy arms that extend all around the room and my students are in their protection. My energy flows through the whole room. I don't sit back and let things happen. I am confident and in control.

If you are nervous before class, especially if you are new to teaching or if it is the first day meeting new students, that is okay. I am still a bit nervous when I meet a new class. Will they like me? Will they enjoy what I have planned for them? What challenges will I face? These are all things that go through my mind. However, I never linger on these thoughts. I know they are there, but I leave them in the back of my mind and go forward with confidence. I know I am prepared and I always give the best class I can. If someone doesn't like it, so be it. Don't give in to any negative thoughts. Go into your class expecting everything will be fine. If you are prepared, it will be fine. You may have a road bump here or there but that is to be expected. You will deal with any issues when they come up. Let's talk about what exactly you can do to let everyone know you own your space.

The students need to respect your space. This means turning their listening ears on right away when they come into class. There is no running around in the classroom before or during your class. They must also keep their hands to themselves. This means they need to respect your things, such as your papers, music, props, etc. Respecting the other students' bodies and the teacher's body is also a must.

Therefore, when you greet the students give them directions as to what to do right away. Again, this is your room and they have to respect it. Tell them happily and excitedly to sit quietly with you or on specific spots and tell them what you have planned for them in class. This way, they are more willing to sit quietly because they are excited for what is coming.

If you appear in charge and confident, this will do several

things:

* The parents will see you are capable and will feel more comfortable leaving their children with you.
* The children will see you are in control and will be more willing to listen during class.
* There will be less chance of injuries from students running around.

The students are in my care at all times. I am in charge of all aspects of my class including the students' safety and well-being as well as their behavior. Most of all, I am in charge of whether or not the class has fun! Think of yourself as a magician creating a wonderful magical experience for the students!

Right before the start of class you have the opportunity to set the tone for your class. By owning your dance space and reaching out to your families, you will have the confidence and control you need to be successful.

Chapter 2 "Pointes" to Remember

* Be On Time
* Be Happy!
* Greet Your Students
* Show Interest in Your Students
* Be in Communication With Parents
* Own Your Dance Space

Chapter 3

How to Run Your Class

We just talked about what to do before class begins to lead the way to a great class. So now what? What do you do during your class? In this section, we will talk about the different parts of your class from start to finish. We will talk about how the class flows and how you and the students should participate in the activities.

Learn the Students' Names Quickly

Learn the students' names as quickly as possible. This is something I have become very good at through practice. It is much easier to keep control over a class if you know each child's name.

I learned very early on if a child is not paying attention

saying, "Hey you!" doesn't cut it. The child will not turn to look at you unless you use their name. If one student is not listening it will make it harder for you to run your class smoothly. Once one child is not listening more may follow.

Using name tags is a great solution. This way, on the first day of class you can go through your class without having to think about remembering names. Instead you can concentrate on what you will be teaching. However, I will give you some tips about what to do if you don't have name tags on hand.

When I am teaching a new group of students, I have them tell me their names often. However, taking time out of class to stop and ask names can lose the class's attention. If you have a small class this is not as much of an issue, but with a full class of preschoolers, you don't want to stop and take time out of class to ask their names very often. There are some special times I will try to ask the children's names throughout class.

First, I make sure I have the class roster with me at the beginning of class. When the children come into the room I introduce myself to the parents and the children, and ask for each child's name. Seeing the name on the list along with the child's face will help me remember their names. I sometimes then write a description of what the child looks like by their name. This is especially helpful if I have more than one child with the same name in a class.

The next thing I will do is try to memorize the students' names before class begins. If we have some time as we are waiting for the other children to arrive, I will ask each child their name and maybe what their favorite color, food or character in a story is.

Another time I ask the students' names is when we are stretching or playing creative games. It is a good idea to play games while you stretch to make it more interesting for the preschooler. When you are stretching the students are sitting down and you can ask them questions about the game you are playing. You can also try this before an activity. If you are pretending to be princesses going on an adventure you can ask where each princess wants to go, or what the princess's horse's name is etc. I say to the children, "Please tell us your name and what your horse's name is?" They will respond and I will say, "Great! Clare's horse's name is Buttercup!" The more repetition I can have the better.

I also take the opportunity to ask the students' names when we practice leaps or take turns going under the parachute. I will say to whoever is next in line, "What is your name? Okay, now it's Sarah's turn!"

Whenever I feel I can ask the students' names and hold the class's attention at the same time, I will. You will have a much easier class and impress parents if you learn names quickly.

Have Big Energy

Throughout your entire class you should have a lot of energy. The children really feed off of you. Whether you are happy and energetic or distracted and tired they will follow suit. Make sure you dance and talk with a lot of energy in order for you to have a fun and productive class.

I mentioned earlier I teach with more of a calm and controlled mannerism. This however, does not mean I don't have a lot of energy. When I dance, I dance big! I reach and stretch as high as I can, I jump and leap big, and I chassé with enthusiasm. I know if I mark my movement, my students will too. I need to set a good example of how to dance completely.

During each of my pregnancies it was not possible for me to dance as big as I wanted to. I was advised by my doctor not to jump (it was uncomfortable anyway) and I couldn't touch my toes! My preschool students didn't understand this. If I didn't jump very high, they didn't. If I didn't touch my toes, they didn't. I had to remind them many times to dance bigger than I danced. I had to use more vocal commands to tell them what to do. It was a challenge, but with my voice, my facial expressions and the parts of my body that could still move big, I got through those times.

Have you ever had a day where you were tired or maybe had a cold and your energy wasn't as high as usual? Or maybe a day where you felt really good and you could teach all day! Did you notice how your students responded? You probably noticed on the days you were feeling good your classes were easier to teach and everyone had a better time. If you are happy and energetic your students will be too and respond in a much more positive way!

Another factor that helps keep the energy of class going is during class I am in constant communication with my students. I feel like I am talking all the time. Either I am giving directions, giving encouragement, or telling funny jokes. This keeps the energy up and the class flowing smoothly.

Preschoolers will mimic your energy. This is actually true for any age group you teach. As teachers, we need to be fully present at each class and dance and talk with full energy in order to have the best class we can.

Start Class With Something Interesting

It is a good idea to start your class with something different and interesting. How are you going to grab your students' attention? Don't start practicing pliés over and over. Start with something preschool friendly.

When I teach a ballet class to little ones I always start with an upbeat song to encourage my students to jump and move around. It is great to see the children's huge smiles when they skip and chassé. They see this is going to be a fun class right away. They also start to trust me right away because they are having fun. Usually shy children will come out of their shells as well when fun music is played.

Reading a short story or part of a story is also something I like to do at the beginning of class. Let's continue with the example of "Twinkle Twinkle Little Star". You could find a book about stars that is appropriate for preschoolers. If it is a short book, you could read the whole book at the start of class. If the book is longer, read a few pages at the start of each class for a few weeks. Remember not to spend too long reading however. You are teaching a dance class!

Another option is to give the students props. For example, start with a parachute game or give the students stuffed animals to dance with. Props will also help shy children or children that need help focusing join the class easier. I will go into how to deal with shy or unfocused children later in this book.

Make sure you capture the students' attention right away. This way, the children will be excited for what you have coming up next!

Mix Up the Class

Be sure you are mixing things up during your class. Don't spend too much time on one activity or one type of activity. Preschoolers have short attention spans and can't handle one activity for a long time.

After you are finished warming up, have the students move around or bring in props. If you are working on a dance, try not to work on a second dance right away. Practice leaps or jumps, bring out a parachute or play a creative movement game. Always keep things moving and changing.

Here is an example of how I run a 45 minute pre-ballet class:

* Warm up – briefly introduce steps, jump around, stretch, etc.
* Practice a dance
* Play a creative movement game
* Play a creative game with props

*   Practice another dance
*   Practice leaps or jumps
*   Play another creative movement game

This is just one example. You can switch up the order any way you choose. You should also keep in mind the class's energy level and attention span. Some days you will not be able to do two dances and others you may be able to do three. Some days the students will need to run around more and others they may be able to focus more. Be prepared to go with the flow. Let's talk more about that now.

Be Willing to Change Your Plan

In a preschool dance class, you never know what may happen. The students may be shy one day and super excited the next. If you teach more than one class, each class could also be very different. A class could also change their mood half way through.

What if you notice the class needs something different than what you have already planned? And how do you know if your class needs a change?

Example:

You just finished a dance with your class and you planned to have the students sit down and practice leaps one at a time. On this day however, you notice the students are looking a little unfocused and if you have them sit down the energy of the class might crash. What do you do?

I have already mentioned why it is so important to know your material. The choreography or games you play should be second nature in order for you to think about all the other things you need to teach. Not only are you teaching steps, you are watching the students' behavior, noticing if they are having fun and thinking about what you are going to have them do next. We as teachers have a lot on our plates!

If you have noticed the class's energy is a bit low what should you do? You will need to quickly change your plan to something more upbeat. Instead of having the children sit, it may be time for a creative movement game that has everyone moving around. You could choose a game you had planned to save for later or incorporate leaps into a game that has everybody moving at the same time.

What if you need the children to focus on a dance in order to prepare them for a show and you are having trouble keeping their attention? When I finish an activity, I not only notice the mood of my class, but I also keep in mind what I want them to learn that day. If we are preparing for a performance, they do need to practice their dances. I have the children practice their dances, but fit creative games in between each dance in order to keep their attention for the whole class. If you are only doing one dance for the show, have the children practice the dance at the beginning of class and then after a few games have them practice the dance again at the end of class if needed. This way, they can practice their dances without becoming bored and when it is performance time the children will be ready. If they are particularly focused one day then you could practice the dance right away again and take advantage of their attention. Reward them with a creative game afterwards.

Always remember, if you feel as if you practiced the dance one more time you would completely lose your class, don't worry about it. Move on. These are preschoolers. We don't need to and don't want to drill them. They will follow you in a show anyway and do just fine! Just be willing to go with the flow. Of course we want the children to follow the class plan but never force it. We don't want to lose their focus and we also don't want them to dislike the class. Do your best and remember to have fun!

Use Props

Props are very helpful in a class with children of all ages. Props bring something new and different to the class, spark creativity and help develop motor skills.

For example, children can use instruments in class. Shakers are a great companion to dance around with and are a perfect beginning musical instrument. Many other musical instruments can be used in class as well, such as drums, bells or sticks (be careful not to run around with sticks or poke anyone). You can make an orchestra or a marching band. Not only are the children using their small and large motor skills, but they are also learning the beginnings of rhythm and musicality.

Other props such as stuffed animals or bean bags are good for hand eye coordination. Students can jump or leap over them. They can be gently tossed or balanced on different body parts while trying to dance at the same time. Animals are also great to use in creative games that use the imagination.

Parachutes are my favorite. The students can shake them up and down, fast or slow. They can also dance under them. We can even pretend they are big flowers or tents and use them in creative activities.

There are so many possibilities when using props. They help add spice to a class and the students love them! For more information about using props in your classes check out my ebook, *Creative Movement Games for Preschoolers: Incorporating Props* which is available on Amazon.

Use Your Music

It is so important to use your music. Putting music together with dance steps helps children learn rhythm and musicality. It has been proven exposing children to music improves such things as brainpower, creativity and social skills. Basically, music helps brain development just like dance. This is why artists know how important dance and music education is to our young people and we need to do what we can to keep them alive!

Over the years, I have witnessed a few teachers who simply put their music on and don't actually use it. They dance as if it was not even there. When the music ends they keep going. They don't dance to the rhythms or the nuances of the music. It just runs on and on and there is no clear use for it.

For me, I think that is confusing for students. If the music is independent of the dance there is no cohesion. The child will not learn to connect the two together. When children are very young they can already express the feelings of the music they hear with their bodies. If a child hears fast music, they will dance fast. If they hear slow music, they will dance slow. They are very perceptive. Having students move with different kinds of music is a good creative movement exercise for children as well.

Music can set the mood for your class and it can be used in exercises. Do you want your class to jump around like bunnies or pretend to be floating snowflakes in the wind. What kind of music can you use to create a feeling you want? Sometimes we want our classes jumping with excitement and big smiles. Other times we may want our students to be curious, exploratory and graceful. Classical music is great for playing pretend. We can listen and dance to different nuances and details. There are so many creative feelings to explore. One piece of classical music can switch from one feeling to the next to create many possibilities for storytelling through dance!

If you are teaching chassés, skips or any movement that is quick, make sure to use a piece of music with a quicker pace. Any music meant for barre exercises will work with an appropriate tempo. You could also use any popular song for children with an upbeat tempo. Preschoolers may not be able to move on the beat but they should be exposed to the correct music in order to start to connect the two together. This way, learning to move to the beat of the music will come quicker.

Dancers need to learn to listen to music. They need to learn to have it flow through them in order to be expressive when dancing. Learning to hear the rhythms and moods of a particular piece of music is essential in learning to dance. This needs to be taught in a dance class and not be neglected. Technique is important but learning to express a piece of music through dance will help students also become successful storytellers when performing for an audience.

Children love music. Using music appropriately in your classes will not only help the students learn ballet steps more efficiently but will stimulate their minds to benefit anything else they wish to do!

Follow the Leader

Perform activities with your students. This take a lot of energy, but the more you actively teach preschoolers, the more you will see how they mimic you and your energy and learn faster. It is actually quite interesting how true this is.

In all my years of teaching and taking classes I have experienced many different teaching styles. Some teachers give it their all and dance the whole class with their students while others give directions and watch.

The first way is the better choice, in my opinion, for students of all ages. Students do need to learn to stand on their own but it is so beneficial for dancers to not only learn what a step is but to see a professional execute that step. We may work on memorization of steps in a preschool class but it is not as important. Preschool students have trouble following directions when just being told to do something. They truly need someone to follow. Once they are used to your style and activities, you can let them perform more by themselves. However, you will always need to perform dances and activities with more structured choreography with your students. You can let them play creative games by themselves, such as pretending to be animals, for example. However again, you must notice how the class is responding. Are they jumping right into being animals or are they looking at you a bit confused. If they are not jumping right in, you will have to demonstrate and participate. Some students will have no problem dancing and creating without you but other students may be more shy or unsure. They will need to see you move in order to feel comfortable. If you are not leading them the energy of the class may drop as well. Or the children will become distracted. You as the leader set the direction for the class. Without that, the class may quickly lose focus.

This point is very important in keeping the energy up in your class. Students need a high energy and positive leader to lead them. Always notice how your class responds to your energy and if you need to participate more. Yes, part of dancing is learning how to dance without the teacher, but again these are preschoolers and you shouldn't worry too much about that at this point. Have fun right along with your students!

Have the Students Add to the Activities

Have the children add to your activities in class. This way, they will feel they are a bigger part of the class. Preschoolers love to help their teachers. It also makes them feel special because they have the opportunity to say or do something all by themselves in front of the other students.

For example, I know a popular stretch is to sit with feet together in "butterfly position". The students can all have a turn to say where they want their butterfly to fly.

Another example is you can ask the children questions about the song they are dancing to. If you are doing a dance to "Twinkle Twinkle Little Star", you can ask each child what they would wish for if they were to wish on a star?

You can also ask children questions during an activity. Act out different animals and ask each child what animal they want to be. Or you can play a fairy game and ask each child to describe their dress, wand, house, etc.

When playing a creative game you can have the children sit and ask them to dance one at a time. I love to do this in my classes. It is so much fun so see how each student expresses themselves. They each have their own style. Some students love to jump and bounce and others love to move smoothly and gracefully. It is a good reminder we all have our own styles.

If you have a very young class, with mostly three year olds, or just a very high energy class, you may not be able to stop and ask a lot of questions. You will have to judge if you can take the time or not. Sometimes it is best to go right into dancing in order to not lose the students' attention. But it is fun for them to add to the class. It is also fun to hear the wonderful and sometimes hilarious ideas they come up with!

End Each Class With a Reward

It is a good idea to gather the students together and end each class with a reward for a job well done. Students will then have a positive memory of not only how much fun they had in class but that their teacher gave them something extra special.

You can reward your students by giving them a simple sticker or stamp at the end of class. You will be amazed at how big of a deal something this small is to a preschooler. This simple reward accomplishes three things: 1) It easily gathers your class together which creates an organized conclusion to the class. 2) It reinforces the reason for your rules. 3) It makes the children feel good!

Remind the students occasionally as to why they receive stamps and / or stickers at the end of each class. Unless you tell them why, a preschooler will not understand what they are for. Let them know they are receiving stamps for being good listeners. Tell them they did a great job in class and now it is time for stamps! Then I tell them they have to sit like a pretzel or criss-cross apple sauce with one hand on top of their head. When everyone is sitting quietly like a pretzel with one hand on their head, I will go around and put a stamp on each child's hand. Each child must sit quietly and wait until everyone has a stamp before we leave the room. I think it is polite to have everyone wait for their friends and this way we can leave together in an organized fashion.

Now, not only are your students excited because they received a stamp, but your whole class is sitting quietly when the parents come pick them up. The parents will be very impressed at how calm the class is.

At the end of your sessions, you can even give your students a bigger reward such as a special sticker, little toy or certificate. This will show them how much you appreciated having them in your class, and make them feel extra special!

How you structure your class and how you act in your class will have a huge impact on how your class runs. You should have a definite plan from start to finish. This way, all you will have to do is carry out your plan. Of course plans can change depending on your students, however if you are prepared and have a back-up, any little change will not be an issue. Let's now go a bit deeper and talk about teaching dance to your preschool students.

Chapter 3 "Pointes" to Remember

* Learn the Students' Names
* Have Big Energy
* Start Class With Something Interesting
* Mix Up the Class

* Be Willing to Change Your Plan
* Use Props
* Use Your Music
* Follow the Leader
* Have the Students Add to the Activities
* End Each Class With a Reward

Chapter 4

How to Teach Dance to Preschoolers

E ven though we are working with preschoolers, we still can teach steps and choreography. They may not learn the entire *Nutcracker*, however they can still learn a few things. Always keep in mind it is important the children learn through creativity and encouragement. By using imagination and positive reinforcement your students will impress!

Teaching Steps

How do you teach ballet steps to preschoolers? Remember preschoolers learn differently than other age groups. You do not want to drill steps and dances with the children each class. Be creative.

Example:

A teacher had her students practice their dances over and over again without music. She had a lot of trouble keeping the students' attention, and nobody was having fun. Not long after I had the opportunity to sub her class. When I subbed this teacher's class the children did not know their dances or steps. However, I was not surprised. Why is this?

My students know their steps and I never drill them. Preschoolers do not learn by repeating steps over and over again. This is the biggest secret to teaching a preschool ballet class. They are a different kind of learner. I quickly go over a few steps with the children after I have had them jumping around in our warm-up at the beginning of class. Then, I will go over a couple steps before each dance that might be new or just need practicing. I do this though, not only so they learn, but in order for the steps to look familiar when they come up in the dance. At the end of class, after I gather them for stamps, I will quiz the students on what steps we learned that day. They are always excited to show me what they remember. We don't want to drill steps, but we also don't want the students to become frustrated because the class is going too fast for them and they don't know what is happening. In both instances, you will lose their attention and enthusiasm. Talk about the steps a little bit at different points in the class and they will learn.

Another point is to teach the ballet steps in a creative way. For example, how can the children learn first position? I have heard teachers call first position "pizza feet" or the letter "V". You could also ask the children to use their magic fingers or magic wands to open their toes. What about doing a plié? How can you make that fun? Can we make a diamond or pretend to open a window with our knees? Can you turn performing the steps into a game? You can use your imagination for any ballet step. When your students are seeing the same steps week after week in a fun way, they will learn and remember.

Positive reinforcement is also a great tool to use to teach preschoolers. Praise them often when they complete a skill even if it is not perfect. At this age we first want them to perform in any way they are able. Then they should receive a compliment for simply trying. After you have established they are doing well you can then add some technique. For example, when we pretend to dip our toes in a pond doing tendus I will say, "When we dip our toes into the pond let's make sure we point them all the way! Great job!"

In chapter two I mentioned the steps I feel preschool students can handle. They won't be perfect but they are doable at this age. Again they are first position, second position, plié, relevé, tendu, passé and arabesque. There are a few others I will add in each session to mix it up. I want to keep the class interesting for both old and new students all year round.

If you follow what I have illustrated above, your preschool students will learn ballet steps. Not only will they learn them but they will associate performing each step with a fun, creative game they will want to do again and again! This is how to teach preschoolers ballet steps.

Teaching Choreography

Teaching Choreography to young students is exciting and so much fun! I love seeing preschoolers act out creative songs with passion and energy. However there are a couple things that need to be considered. If you go over too much choreography at once they will become bored. If you do not demonstrate enough, they may become frustrated because they don't know what you are doing. You must find a balance.

There are a couple different ways you can teach choreography to preschoolers. If you teach at a studio where students have many months to prepare you can approach choreography differently than if you teach in a recreational program that only runs a few weeks. At a studio the students may also need to be more polished than in a recreational program. Therefore we may teach the choreography a bit different for each. In the end, for both instances, the choreography still needs to be creative and fun.

When I have to prepare students for a big recital, and we have many weeks or months before the show, I teach the choreography for our dance little by little every week. I teach the first verse one week, then add the chorus the next week, and so on until the dance is finished and we can just run it. I will probably have the children run the section we have worked on that day two or three times if I can tell they can handle it. In this instance, I want the choreography to be clear and well learned. I don't want to just skim over it. Just covering a little each week will help keep the students interested. Then we also have more time for creative games.

As for a recreational program with a shorter session, I will teach just the first verse of choreography before I turn on the music. Then, we will dance the whole song with music and they can follow me for the rest of the song. Or, if there are new or tricky steps I will go over them first before we dance the whole song with music. The students are happy to follow along if you are upbeat and energetic. During the dance you should also try to sing the song or talk about what you are doing at the same time. Not only that, but be able to quickly call out what is coming next. This is why it is very important to know your dances. You have so many things to think about when you are teaching, as I have already mentioned. This way, the children will be ready and able to follow you. If you have good, upbeat energy and you call out what they are going to do before they do it, everything will be fine.

This is another secret I have learned along the way. Preschool students will follow you no matter what you do. If you just turn on the music to a dance and start dancing, they will follow you. Like I always say you must dance big and call out what they should be doing in order for this to work.

Example:

I recently had to sub a recreational class for one of my teachers. Even though all of my teachers teach the same curriculum in our Wish Upon a Ballet™ classes, we all of course do not teach the dances exactly the same way. On this day it was the last day of class therefore it was also the in class performance for the parents. Before the performance there was only enough time to run one of the dances with the students. I picked the one that was the most challenging because the dance incorporated props. I crossed my fingers for the show and the students followed me perfectly. We performed three dances for the parents and they followed me very well. I was surprised, even though I knew preschoolers follow their teacher.

If I have a class that is unfocused or if I can see the energy is too high I will also just turn on the music to a dance and have the students follow me. This is a good way to keep from losing your students. Going through the steps and choreography isn't as important for a preschool class as it is for older students. They just want to dance and jump around. They will follow you if necessary.

Another tip is to make sure the choreography is fun and interesting for the students. It shouldn't be all ballet steps. Add some gestures that go with the song. For example, in "Twinkle Twinkle Little Star" can the students make twinkling stars with their fingers? Can they float around like a star in the sky? Tell a story with the song and the children will love it.

Make sure you mix up the steps as well. Have the students perform some tendus and then change it up with some sauté jumps or turns. It also helps if the children can move around at times and not be stuck in one place. Chassé or skip around in a circle. This is also great to learn spacial awareness. I always practice moving around in a circle in my warm-ups. This way I can use circles in my choreography and the students already know what to do. Moving to new places in the room is just as challenging as learning new steps. It does need to be practiced.

Preschoolers will eventually pick up choreography. You just need to be patient. However, at this age don't expect them to do a whole dance all by themselves, especially at a performance. You will always have to be there doing the dance with them. Not only should you be there to remind them of their dances, but just being there makes them feel more secure. You can read more about performing with your students in chapter seven.

Teaching Technique

There are many different beliefs as far as how to teach ballet technique to young children. Some people believe you should teach just as you would teach older children, standing at the barre in turn out. Another side believes preschool children shouldn't stand at the barre or turn out at all, teaching everything in parallel. Some people believe you shouldn't even touch the subject of ballet until children are older.

I believe there is a happy medium. Little children love to pretend to be ballet dancers. Therefore, I think it is okay to teach ballet if you teach responsibly and keep the health of their little bodies in mind. At this age preschoolers do not have the muscle development or the understanding to handle technique. For example, I dance in turn out but I don't force my students to dance in turn out. Preschoolers won't anyway. I show them first position and have them try it, but then I let it go. During the rest of the class their bodies will naturally dance how they dance at this age. They usually won't even notice if they are in turn out or not. You don't have to completely avoid turning out. It is part of our range of motion and touching on it is fine.

However, don't force the preschoolers to stay in turn out. There is plenty of time for that and other more complex technique later.

There are some children too, who want to over turn out. This, however usually happens with older students. Some students also might want to walk on pointe in their soft shoes. We always want to correct students who are performing any step that might hurt them. Don't encourage your students to over extend their bodies. As teaching artists we are not only responsible for teaching them to dance but are responsible for teaching them how to take good care of themselves.

There are some easy elements of technique I do teach my preschool students. We do want the students to stand up tall, point their toes and dance with big energy. Learning to do those things is definitely achievable. It depends on the class but I don't talk about technique much more than that at this age.

Using creativity and games to teach technique is always the way to go. When we plié, for example, I ask the students to open a window with their knees and tell me how the weather is. "Is it cold outside? Oh no! Quick, close your window!" It is a fun exercise my classes never get tired of. It can be cold, hot, rainy, snowy, etc!

Another way I teach technique besides using creativity is to challenge the students in a fun way. To encourage the students to dance big I will say, "who can jump as high as I can?" or "Who can reach up super high?" Preschoolers love a challenge and they love to show you how well they can perform.

Technique can be achieved at the preschool level. Preschoolers can definitely understand how to stand up tall and dance with big energy. Some can also understand how to point their toes or have straight legs in tendu or arabesque. It is fun to see how much they can accomplish when it is taught in a fun way!

Don't Expect Perfection

Preschoolers should not be expected to perform everything correctly. When teaching students of all ages teachers should always be mindful of whether or not the students are having fun and are inspired. We want them to love our classes and leave wanting more! When we expect perfection we risk losing the fun of dance class.

This is especially true for preschool classes. Preschoolers think of dance as purely playtime. It is a place where they can use their imaginations and jump around. They are usually not paying attention to whether they have their steps correct. In fact, they think they already look amazing!

Most preschoolers will not notice if they are not doing a step correctly. However once in a while you will have a preschool student who recognizes they are not quite doing a step right. Then they might become frustrated and not want to participate if they don't feel they are doing well. If that is the case help them the best you can but try to let them know it is fine if they don't have it perfect. For example, most students will be able to perform a chassé starting with either the right foot or left foot. Performing it with the opposite foot might be too tricky. If you see the look of frustration on their face just let the student perform the chassé with the same foot until they feel more confident.

At this stage dance should be all about having fun! We want to inspire the students so they will want to continue in our program. Even if they don't continue we still want them to have fond memorize of dance class. Maybe they will take class or go to see dance performances in the future.

Children learn best through creativity and fun. Of course, every child is different and some may be able to handle a more technical class and still enjoy it. However I don't think it is necessary to teach preschoolers in any way that is not full of imagination. Play and have a great time!

Teaching ballet to preschoolers can be achieved. Through creativity you can teach steps, choreography and a bit of technique and your students will have a wonderful time learning! Students will follow you in class and when it is show time. Of course they will only follow you if you are full of energy and have fun! As I have mentioned before, do not feel as though you have to drill them. There is plenty of time for that if they want to pursue dance more seriously in the future.

Chapter 4 "Pointes" to Remember

* Teach Steps Through Play
* Use Creative Choreography
* Keep Technique Simple
* Don't Expect Perfection

Chapter 5

How to Keep the Class Listening

L ike I have said, teaching preschool dance is completely different than teaching dance to older students. It is an art. The goals are to teach your curriculum and keep the students paying attention to you the whole class while still having fun. How do you keep a preschooler paying attention for your entire class? Whether or not you are able to achieve your objective will depend mostly on how you run your class. If you follow all of the points I have made so far in this book, you will succeed in keeping a well run class the majority of the time. In this chapter, I will go a bit further to insure your success.

First, you will need to understand the mind of the preschooler. If you understand the preschooler you will have more success dealing with them. Second, I will talk about so called "tricks" I use to keep the class listening. Last, I will touch on special situations such as children who are shy or are more likely to test you. If you put these suggestions together along with the material I have already covered, you will be on your way to a great class!

Part 1 ~ Know Your Audience ~ Going Inside the Mind of a Preschooler

In order to be a successful teacher, you have to know your students inside and out. Preschoolers are no exception. In fact, I feel it is even more important to know the preschooler than it is to know the minds of older students. The way the preschooler thinks is different. This is because they are in the very early stages of growth and development. Sometimes they way they process doesn't make sense to those of us that are older. I learned early in my teaching career knowing how the preschooler thinks helped me teach my classes immensely.

Be One Step Ahead

Always anticipate what the students are going to do before they do it. This will come with time and experience. With experience, you will soon see what preschoolers like to do that they should not do in class. Be prepared at each activity for unwanted behavior and remind the students what they should be doing. Here are some examples:

Preschoolers love to run around in an open room like a dance studio if you don't tell them where to be. You need to be prepared and ask them to sit in between activities or be ready to go right into the next activity. This is why I have the students sit with me or on spots immediately when they come into class, because I know they are going to run around if I don't tell them otherwise.

If you take them out of the room for example, to the bathroom, they will want to run down the halls. They will also talk loudly if not reminded to use their inside voices. Remind them, before you go out into the hall, what is expected of them. Have them line up and go over the rules. "How do we go down the hall? We walk in a line and use our inside voices."

Another example is when I use props. I know some preschoolers are going to bang my shakers on the floor or put them in their mouths, therefore I go over the rules before we use them. I also know they will run on top of my parachute and fall down if I don't remind them to stay off of it. Most girls love anything pink, so if they don't get one of my pink scarves they may have a meltdown. If your students get to choose props and you want to avoid meltdowns, have scarves or shakers that are all the same color or just remove the pink ones if you think the students might fight over them.

Become used to being one step ahead of your class. Know what they are going to do before they do it in order to avoid unwanted behavior and potential accidents.

Know What is Fun

This point goes along with the point above. Not only know what the preschooler is going to do before they do it for behavioral and safety reasons, but you need to actually go inside their minds so they have fun! What is fun for the preschooler? What do they like to do? What makes them laugh?

Here are a couple ideas I will share with you. The first one, is again, that preschoolers like to run around. I don't like my students to actually run around in class, therefore I make sure I have them move in other ways. They can chassé, skip, jump, and leap around. Have them move in a way that is related to dance. Make sure they all go around the room in the same direction. If not, there might be a collision! I train my students from day one to all go around the room counter clockwise whenever we chassé or skip around.

Second, preschoolers like to make believe. Girls usually love anything related to princesses, fairies or magic. Superheroes and pirates are also a hit especially if you have boys in the class. Pretending to be animals is great for both boys and girls. Choose activities and dances that relate to subjects children love.

If you have many high energy yet controlled games along with a creative program, you will have a super fun class.

Are Your Students Having Fun?

Once you have created a great curriculum with what you think are many fun and engaging activities, how do you know if your students will enjoy what you have planned? If your students are having fun it will be so much easier to have a smooth and controlled class. They will want to listen to you and will be eager to learn. Here are some ways to tell if your students are having fun.

The way to tell if the students are having fun is if they look attentive. Look at the children's faces. Are they looking at you? Are they smiling? Do their faces look bright? Or are they going off to do their own activity? Ask them questions about the activity. Do they answer you? If they are not paying attention you need to quickly assess what you are doing. Have you spent too long on one activity? Are you moving too slowly? You don't have to necessarily change the activity you are doing. Maybe you just need to raise your energy level. Keep in mind if one student or even a couple students are not listening that doesn't always mean the class is not going well. Preschoolers all have their moments of not listening. Look at the rest of the group. Do you have most of the children's attention? If so, you are probably okay. Just remind the ones who are not following what they should be doing.

If most of the students don't look engaged and simply raising your energy isn't working you may have to change what you are doing. Sometimes groups need to take a break, move around the room, get their sillies out or shake a parachute. Everyone needs a break from time to time, even preschoolers.

Don't just teach your class and go through the curriculum. Always watch the students and be ready to adjust if necessary. If you are teaching the same class to different children, remember all classes will be different. Some classes are quiet and others are more "squiggly". You can't sit and stretch for a long time with a squiggly class. Keep control over your students by not letting their energy take over the class. For shy or quiet groups, energize them by laughing and jumping around. For classes with too much energy, try to channel that energy into an interesting and engaging creative activity.

We always want the children to have fun. I believe this is our biggest job. If your class is fun and controlled your students will come back for more!

Knowing the minds of your preschool students keeps your class moving the in the right direction. What I have given you will keep you one step ahead all the time. Of course, there is much more to be learned. You will have to learn how to read your students on your own through experience.

Part 2 ~ Special Tricks of the Trade

There are a few simple activities and phrases I use that help me teach my classes. I did not invent them. They are used in many preschools. This section may be the most important section in this book. Without these "tricks" my classes would not run as smoothly. Not only do they keep the class listening, but they keep the students happy and feed their self-esteem as well.

Use Dancing Spots

Always giving your students directions will help keep your

classes on track. Preschoolers need directions otherwise they will quickly find their own activity to do. Actually, they really like to know what they are supposed to be doing. It gives them comfort.

Finding a place to be in the room when they enter or when finishing an activity will help the preschooler feel a sense of belonging. If they are new they might be shy and not know what to expect coming into the dance space. Giving them a place to be right away will be calming. They will understand this is where I sit and wait for my next direction. Students who have been to class for a while are also comforted by a specific place to be. They know right away to come in the room and find their spot.

Using tape on the floor is an easy way to make spots for your class. Stickers will also work as well. If you have your own space, you can make more elaborate spots for the children. There are also portable spots for preschool classes. They come in many bright colors and different fun shapes.

Reinforcing going to spots when students come in the room and in between activities will help your class succeed in listening. Preschoolers will learn to sit and be ready for their next instruction. Hopefully after just one class they will understand what to do and you won't even need to say anything. At the next class they will run right in and sit down.

Helpful Phrases

There are many phrases you can use with children to keep the class listening. We don't want to ever tell a child they are "bad". There are no bad children, just undesirable behaviors.

When a child is not paying attention or doing what you have asked, we use the phrase, "listening ears". For example, when a student is not listening you can say, "Sarah, are your listening ears on?" At the beginning of class you can remind the students they all must "Turn on their listening ears". You can make this a game by how you have them "turn on" their ears. They can turn them up like a volume knob and add funny sounds as you are doing this such as "crank, crank, crank!" Or "Whooooop!" Turn as many things into a game as possible. This way, it is not like "Teacher" is constantly scolding them.

Another helpful term children will need to know if they don't already, is using their "inside voices". Screaming or yelling is not allowed in class. Tell a child who is being too loud to use their "inside voice". Screaming or yelling is an "outside voice" and is for outside only. If there is too much talking I tell the students, "Please put a bubble in your mouth!" Then I hold a pretend bubble and show them how to put it in my mouth. This one is very helpful and also fun for the students. It is great to see a whole class with their mouths full of "bubbles"!

Children must also "keep their hands on their own bodies". We don't want children poking at other children. Preschoolers also like to hold hands with their friends. This is very cute, and if it is not distracting I sometimes let it go. However, if you are dancing and they need their arms and hands just nicely tell them to let go. There are times for partners and times for dancing solo.

Using special phrases with your preschoolers will help you succeed in running a great class. These are phrases your students have probably heard in school and will be able to relate to. The more they hear them the faster they will understand and follow along.

Sitting "Criss-Cross Apple Sauce"

This, to me, is huge! When the students are not doing an activity have them sit cross legged. Always, always, always! You can call this, "criss-cross apple sauce", "pretzel sit", "sit and listen position" etc. This way, children learn your expectation is to sit and listen for directions when they are not doing an activity. It is also a great position that doesn't allow a lot of wiggling.

If you don't give your students the direction to sit, the children will most likely run around. Then you will have to work harder to bring them back to class in order to do the next activity. Not only will you lose precious class time, but the children will be less likely to pay attention afterwards. At the beginning of class, gather them and have them sit. When you are between activities have them sit unless you are ready to go right into the next activity. They should always be looking at you and ready to hear what is next.

Children can't just sit however they want either. Sitting cross legged is also the best position because they can't wiggle around as much. Sitting cross legged plants them in one spot so you can teach your class in a much more controlled atmosphere.

When they sit cross legged they also learn they will be rewarded. I have my students practice sitting cross legged when we pick props, for example. The children have to sit quietly like a pretzel in order to be able to pick a prop. Make sure you tell them what you expect. "Okay now everyone sit like a pretzel. When I see you are sitting quietly I will call your name to choose an animal. Oh! Clare is sitting quietly like a pretzel, she can pick an animal. Wow! I love how many of you are sitting so quietly!"

We have already talked about students having to sit cross legged in order to receive a stamp at the end of class. This is the same purpose. We want our students calm, quite and ready for what it next. If they do that, they will be rewarded.

I am firm about this but I also remember not to labor over one or two children who just don't seem to understand. Always keep the class moving and positive. At the age of three, some children have never sat cross legged before. You may actually have to teach them how to do it. If a child doesn't sit like a pretzel, as long as it is not a distraction and you are ready to move on to something else, just move on. Another point is to always make it fun. Don't order the students to sit down. Say something like, "That dance was great everyone! Now who can sit like a pretzel the quickest? Wow! You are all so fast! Let's play a game now!" Remember to always be upbeat and fun to keep your students under control.

I even use criss-cross apple sauce as a game to get students to listen if the class has too much energy. I will say "Okay everyone, sit down criss-cross apple sauce!" Some of the students might listen and sit down while others still may not be paying attention. I will then say, "Oh, I mean stand up! Oh wait I mean sit down! No, stand up!" I do this until everyone is following along and laughing. It is a great way to get the students to listen in a silly way!

Having the children sit criss-cross apple sauce when you are not doing an activity is so important. This not only helps to control your class, but also teaches the students how to respect their teacher. Something that will be beneficial to them when they start school.

Raising Hands

For many of your preschool students this will be the first time they have ever been in a class setting. They may have never heard the phrases, "listening ears" or "criss-cross apple sauce". Another thing we need to teach, is the need to raise their hands quietly when they want to speak.

Because raising their hand is new to this age group, you will have to talk to your students about it often. You can say, "Okay now I have a question for you. If you would like to answer, please raise your hand (show them how by raising your hand) and I will call on you. Now, who can show me a tendu?" What will happen is is actually very cute. Some children will raise their hands, some will shout out "Me! I know!" and others will just stand up and show you their tendu. You will then need to make an example of a child who is quietly raising their hand. "Clare is raising her hand quietly so I will call on her. Clare will you show us your tendu. Wow! Very good! Raise your hand if you would like to go next?"

For some children, it will take a while to understand this. Remember, you are teaching your class not only how to dance but how to be in a class. Be patient and help the younger ones understand by reminding them nicely.

Play the Freeze Dance

The freeze dance is a great tool to use in your classes for more reasons than one. It, of course, can be used as a fun creative movement game but it can also be used to teach steps and as a listening tool. Any game that will also help students listen and learn is wonderful to have on your playlist.

The freeze dance is a great activity for young students. If you are not familiar with the freeze dance it is very simple yet fun and engaging. When music plays we all dance! When the music stops we freeze! There are songs that are specifically meant to play with this activity however you can also use any music and just push pause when you want the students to freeze. I prefer using songs with pauses already in them because then you can dance more easily with your classes. You don't have to be near your music to push pause. I have mentioned how important it is for you to dance along with your students. Not having to be near your music all the time lets you be more free.

The freeze dance is also helpful in teaching and practicing steps. I have mentioned I don't like to drill steps with my students over and over again. When we dance with the music I usually don't let my students dance however they want. This is for a couple reasons. First, if you have shy students they will be reluctant to choose their own steps and jump in. Or students with more energy might run around and not pay attention to others around them. Second, I want to take advantage of this opportunity to teach something. We are not doing this activity in preschool we are in dance class! Let's do special steps! I will have my students chassé or skip. We can take giant steps or baby steps. We can sauté or leap around the space. When we freeze, we can freeze in first position or any other position you might be working on. Sometimes I will ask them to freeze any way they want but it has to be big or silly! I will allow a segment or two for dancing however they want to give them a break but if there are children who are not comfortable choosing their own movement I will still dance so they can follow me.

Finally, the last reason I love this activity is now my students are used to the word, "Freeze!". When we are doing choreography, playing another game or anytime I want my students to quickly stop what they are doing I can say with enthusiasm, "Freeze!" I also make a big X with my body so the word is connected with a movement and it is more noticeable. They all will then make an X and freeze as well. This is much easier and more fun than saying stop. It only works if you have enough energy to get them listening.

Games can be a wonderful tool to not only have fun with but to use to help our students listen. We try our best to keep the fun continue throughout the whole class. Whether we are playing or listening. Having fun is the best way to go.

Keep the Class Positive

Let's talk more about keeping the class positive. It is very important to have a fun upbeat class. Preschoolers only think about whether they are having fun or not in a class. They will not think, "I'm am learning ballet and it won't always be fun, but I should do it anyway because it is good for me." Keeping the class positive is the best way to keep your students learning and it feeds your students' self-esteem as well.

Previously I mentioned the teacher who was very concerned

the students were not listening and doing every single step exactly the way she did. Because of this the class was not fun. The more she scolded them for not listening, the more they didn't listen. It was a downward spiral. The class was bogged down by negativity. Let me tell you now, expecting preschoolers to do everything right is not a reasonable expectation. Your goal should be that everyone listens to you all the time but if a child is not giving you their full attention and it is not distracting to the other children, then that is not a big deal from time to time. Preschoolers are easily distracted. They may pay attention to something else for a few seconds and then dance with you again.

Whatever the case, you need to keep the class positive. Of course we want to keep the students on track. They can't go off and do whatever they want to for long. If they are distracted, we do need to bring them back in class. How do you accomplish that and keep the class listening in a positive way?

First, make sure you are positive right away at the beginning of class. Say things such as:

"Yay! let's go!"

"This is so much fun!"

"Who can jump as high as me?"

When a child is not listening and I need them to come back to class quickly, I first use phrases to try and excite them. Here are some examples:

"Sarah, show me how high you can jump. Wow, that's great! Everyone show me how high you can jump!"

"Look how high James can reach his arms up! Who else can reach that high?"

"Sarah, what are my feet doing? Show me your tendu. That's great!"

If they still don't jump in, I will ask if they want to dance by me, or hold my hand if it looks like they are shy. If they just want to do their own activity I will say happily:

"Who can turn their listening ears on super high? Great!

Come on! Let's chassé!"

Always go to creativity if nothing else works. A creative story or idea works almost every time.

"Do you see that shooting star? We have to chassé to chase it! If you catch it, you can make a wish!"

Don't stop the class and focus on a child that is not listening for too long. You will soon lose the other children and then no one will be listening. Try to encourage the children to dance and participate through positive encouragement.

Being positive and raising your energy works 90% of the time. It definitely works for those students who are distracted or bored. If you have an especially shy child or a child trying to be difficult, you will have to dig deeper. We will talk about those instances at the end of this chapter.

Keep the Class Moving

Preschoolers have short attention spans. Therefore, in a preschool class, you need to move through your activities quickly. When you are about to finish one activity, you should already be thinking about what you are going to do next. There is little time for thinking in between activities. You can't ever finish an activity, turn your back to the students and either look at notes for a long time or scroll through your playlist wondering what song you should play next.

I am always thinking ahead about what I am going to do next. This way, when the activity is over, I can give immediate directions to my students. I have taught for so many years I can do this automatically. Thinking too much between activities will lose your students. If you need to write down the activities you would like to do for that day, it is okay to quickly go to your notes and look at what you have planned next if you can't remember. I would just talk to your students at the same time. Tell them to sit down and ask them questions about the dance or activity they just finished. Keep talking and don't ignore them. Once you have figured out what you will be doing next, quickly give directions.

What do you decide to do next? If you have made a plan that is already thought out, you can simply follow your plan. This is the best way to run a class. Have your music set up so you don't have to find songs. All of the songs you would like to use for class can be on a playlist ready to go. Then you can just go over to it, look at what you have, give directions and push play.

Young children cannot be left to do their own activity for long periods. If you don't give them directions they will find something else to do very quickly. Always be on top of what is coming next in your class in order for you to stay in control.

Don't Ask Yes or No Questions

Don't ask the students whether they want to do an activity or not. Preschoolers are learning to be independent human beings. Therefore, when you ask them if they want to do a particular dance or creative movement game they may say no for no reason.

When you ask preschoolers if they want to do an activity and they say no, then you will have to convince them to do what it is you want. This may cause conflict. Another example of what may happen is some students may want to do the activity and others may not. Then the person that doesn't get their way is disappointed.

It is best to tell the children what activity you would like to do with a fun upbeat attitude. "Okay class! Now, let's sit down criss-cross apple sauce and we can do our leaps one at a time!" Then you will not have to deal with children pouting when you tell them what is happening next. Older children may fuss about certain activities but preschoolers rarely do. Preschoolers are more willing to go with the flow if you make an activity sound like fun. This way, you will continue to keep the class positive. Remember, we want to keep our classes positive as much as possible. Be confident in the choices you make for your classes. You may think offering choices to the students will make them happy, but in reality what makes children happy is when their teacher is in charge.

Give Warnings

I don't give time-outs or take stickers or stamps away at the end of class anymore. Even in the past I rarely had a student where I needed to go to this extreme. However, if you have a student you feel needs something more to keep their attention, please give them a warning first.

Example:

A three year old student is having a great time in dance class on a particular day. She is laughing and carrying on with another student and thinks this is the best dance day ever! At the end of class she is told she wasn't being a good listener that day and did not earn the treat the teacher brought for everyone. The child is devastated! She doesn't understand what she did wrong. She thought the class was a lot of fun. Why was she being punished?

This student was not listening in class and did not know it. The teacher should have first warned the child when she started acting up and told her she would not receive a treat at the end of class if she didn't listen. It is hard for any child to know what is expected of them when a teacher does not explain it. This is especially true for preschoolers who are still learning how to behave in a class. Give your students warnings before you discipline them.

This leads us to the next point...

(The child in this story was me years ago. Yes, I am still upset I didn't get my Tootsie Roll!)

Have Clear Expectations

Your students need to know what you expect from them. This way, they can live up to your expectations. Either let your students know your rules right away at the beginning of class or whenever certain situations come up.

You could go over a few rules at the beginning of every class as part of your welcome. Get the kids to say them enthusiastically along with you. You could even make a game of it. Don't overwhelm the students, however. If you want to go over any rules, go over them quickly and move on. "Let's sit on a spot, turn on our listening ears and have fun!"

Generally, I bring up my rules when they come up. If a child is not listening, I will talk to the whole class about being a good listener. When I take out my props, I will tell the whole class about how to treat them. I let my students know about my rules on an as needed basis.

The children will also know your expectations by the way you act and run the class. If you are well organized and treat everyone with respect they will follow.

If my teacher would have addressed my behavior right away in the story I shared in the last section, I would have known what she expected from me. Hopefully I would have been a good listener! However, she let it go on and never said a word. To be fair, this was a long time ago and I think she was a young teacher. I know I have made my share of mistakes in my teaching career as well. We all can learn from it.

Giving your students your expectations right away will keep your class on track. Students like to know what is expected of them in a class and want to do a great job for their teacher. When they understand what is appropriate they will listen, follow you and pay attention. Everyone will be happier and the students will be free to learn.

Part 3 ~ If You Are Still Having Trouble ~ Special Situations

Sometimes it seems no matter what you have done, one or more children just won't listen. In this section we will talk about what to do in special situations.

Be a Detective

If you have done all of the above and you still have a child that won't listen, you will have to be a detective. What do I mean by this? Can you actually figure out why the student is not listening? Are they shy? Bored? Distracted? Or are they just trying to be difficult? Maybe they are just very young and being in a class is a new experience for them. Maybe this is their first dance class and they are so excited they can't stand still! It might take the student a few weeks to catch on. However, if you can figure out the situation you may be able to solve the problem. Here are some ideas that might help you when you have tried all of the above.

Don't Be Afraid to Question Yourself

If one or more of your students is not listening, you first need to look at what you are doing. Don't ever be afraid to stop and look at yourself to see if you are the reason your class is not paying attention. It could be a very simple adjustment on your part that makes your class run smoother.

Remember the instructor that I spoke of in the section about teaching steps? She was trying over and over again to have the students perform a perfect tendu and it just wasn't working. She kept telling them they were doing it incorrectly and they were tuning out.

When I watched this class to try and help the teacher, the problem was easy to identify. The teacher expected too much from her students. She was drilling the dances without music over and over until she thought the students had each step correct. The class was boring and not preschool friendly. When I approached her about the fact that her class should be more upbeat, fun and not so serious the teacher was surprised. She thought the issue was the students. She didn't think she was part of the problem.

I have witnessed this before with classes of all ages. Teachers will complain their students don't listen when it is the way the instructor is trying to get them to listen that is actually the problem.

You must be able to take a look at yourself if your class isn't running smoothly. Don't feel you have to be perfect all the time. We can all learn new things that will help us become better at what we do. Sometimes I feel teachers are afraid to reach out and ask for help. That asking for help means they are not doing well. When a teacher asks me for help it makes me feel they really care about what is best for their students. Not only do they care about their students but they also care about themselves. When our classes run smoothly we can relax and have fun too!

Was the above teacher's class "squiggly"? Yes it was. There were a couple of very young children in the class that needed to learn how to be in a class. The next week I had a chance to teach the class to show the teacher what I would change. I changed just a few things and was able to run everything smoothly.

What did I do to change the students' behavior? First, I kept the class positive. We didn't dwell on those students that were more of a challenge to persuade to participate. Second, I chose high energy activities and acted as if whatever activity we were doing was the most fun I had ever had. When children see you having fun they will most likely join in. Third, I offered the students who were not listening a chance to hold my hand while we danced. This immediately fixed the problem. The students jumped right in and danced with me. Other times the younger girls just needed to watch for a moment before they jumped in. I found the class a challenge, but not anything that could not be handled. When I taught, we had a great time and completed all of the materials I had planned for the day. Most of all, the students had a great time.

Don't ever have the attitude, "Oh this class just doesn't listen! They don't do anything I ask." Whatever attitude you have your students will have. Be fun as well as in charge and believe you will figure it out.

What if however, you *still* have a child that won't listen?

The Child that Just Won't Listen

If you have tried all of the above and a child still will not listen, then you will need to dig a bit deeper. Again, put on your detective hat. Have you ruled out bored, shy, or distracted? If so, are they just having a bad day? Are they trying to test you?

You will have a child every now and then that just doesn't want to participate for whatever reason. Maybe they don't like structure, they don't like to dance, they are tired, having a bad day, or there could be issues at home. Remember no child is bad. There is always a reason for undesirable behavior even if the reason is they are three years old! You may not be able to figure it out. But it is your job to try and try again.

Example #1:

In the previous story with the class that was more of a challenge, there was an adorable little girl who was the ring leader. I had to pay more attention to her listening ears than the other children when I taught the class. She danced when she was able to hold my hand or had a chance to watch me for a minute before jumping in.

I was able to dance with this class for their final performance and the reason she was more of a handful was obvious. She spent a lot of the time during the show with her finger in her nose. Normally I would have tried to whisper to her to take it out. However her family thought it was hysterical. So I let it go. I now understood why she was more, let's say "carefree" in class. Her family encouraged her behavior. If her parents didn't mind then I didn't mind. She wasn't distracting to the other children during the performance, so it wasn't that big of a deal. But I now understood why she behaved like she did.

Example #2:

During my first year of teaching, I taught for a program that offered dance classes in preschools. At one preschool I had a student who was very difficult. She didn't listen much and a lot of the class was focused on her listening ears. I had to talk to her preschool teacher often about her listening ears. I was very frustrated and dreaded this particular class. Eventually, I found out from her teacher her parents were going through a divorce. This put things in a new light. I wish I would've known that sooner. Even though knowing this information didn't change her behavior, it did give me some more understanding and patience with her and the class. Maybe instead of a time-out she just needed a hug.

There is always a reason why a child misbehaves. Even if you can't figure it out, be understanding to the child and do your best.

When you have a child that is not listening try the ideas previously mentioned:

* Raise your energy level
* Offer to have the student stand by you or hold your hand
* Use the key phrases in the listening section
* Change your activity
* Move quickly from one activity to the next
* Use props
* Look at yourself

If none of these work and the child is being distracting and negative, you will have to go over to them, get down to their level and use your "mom voice" (or dad voice). I learned this from another teacher my first year of teaching. We all know the "mom voice". It is a serious, deeper voice. However, it is not yelling it is calm and in control. You should never yell at your class. Do not tower over the child and scold them. Kneel down to be at their level and tell them seriously but not angrily, "Sarah, you need to turn on your listening ears right now so we can all have fun and play this game." This works very well. Usually you will have their attention at least for a little while. You may have to remind them a couple times. Rarely have I had a situation where I have had to go further than this.

Parents can also be a good resource for you when you are having trouble with their child. You can ask parents to remind their children at home or on the way to class to turn their listening ears on in dance class. Approach parents with care. Parents don't want to hear their child is not listening and can sometimes get defensive. Hopefully they will be understanding and happy to help you out.

Preschoolers really don't want to be difficult or try to manipulate their teachers. Generally, they just want to have fun, and if they are being disruptive they have found another way to have fun. The same way you need to teach them how to plié, you also need to teach them how to behave in a class. That is part of the job of a preschool dance teacher. Many of your students will not have ever been in another class situation before. They need to learn how to behave. I always tell my teachers the first day of class can be the most challenging. However once the students are familiar with you and how your class is run, you will have a much easier time. If your class is super fun you should have very little problems.

Positive Reinforcement

Earlier in my teaching career when I had a student that would not listen well I would use time-outs or I would not give that child a sticker or stamp at the end of class. I don't use either of these methods anymore. Now I am a more skilled teacher and I am more able to keep my students engaged and having fun so they are not as easily distracted.

Of course I do still have a student who does not listen from time to time for whatever reason. Nobody is perfect. I am not and neither are my students so we can't have a perfect class every time. Instead of punishing a student I now use positive reinforcement. I have mentioned that keeping the class positive is very important. We want everyone to think our class is fun and leave them wanting more. If we use positive reinforcement it helps to keep that goal.

When trying my best to have a super fun class doesn't work with all the students, I will use stickers or stamps to get the students paying attention. I will say, "If you sit on your spots by the time I count to five I will give you a stamp right now! One, two, three, four...quick you are almost there! Five! You did it! Here is a stamp!" Young children are not able to think about the future. If you want results fast you must give the reward right away. Sometimes waiting for the stamp at the end of class is not enough.

You can also use fun games as the reward. "If we practice

our dance one more time the best we can we can play with the parachute next!" After all my years of teaching I have found that positive reinforcement works much better than negative reinforcement. If you use it effectively your class can keep going in the right direction.

Helping Shy Students

A shy child can be frustrating. Not because I don't have sympathy for a shy child but because I know they could be having fun if they would just come out from behind Mom or Dad. In most of our classes I ask the parents to sit outside of the classroom. However, if a child won't let go of their parent I let my rules relax a bit. I don't force the child away and I tell the parent they can stay in the room and see how things go. The child will usually sit with Mom, Dad or Grandma etc. for the first part of class. Some parents may try to come out and dance with their child to help involve them in class. With some children, however, it may be necessary for the parent to leave. Their child may miss them for a minute and then be just fine. It is important to have an open discussion with the parent and work together to find the best solution for the child.

First, when I have shy student, I try new things right at the beginning of class. For example, I will ask if the child wants to sit with me when I am taking attendance. If just sitting with me is not enough, I offer them a book to look at, or I give them a prop such as a stuffed animal to hold. Sometimes I throw my whole class plan out the window and start with my parachute right away. Parachutes are great for shy children. Not many children can resist a parachute!

Second, I will let a shy student hold my hand during the dances. I usually start class with a fast warm up song to encourage all the students to start jumping and having fun. We will then chassé or skip around the room. This is a good opportunity to take hold of a shy student and have them skip around with you. They can also stand by you when you are dancing in front of the other children.

Third, I may have a shy child sit by another friendly and upbeat student. Children enjoy being helpers in class. I always have at least one child in class say, "She can sit by me!" This may help a student who doesn't know anyone and just needs a buddy. Having the students introduce themselves at the first class will help everyone become more familiar with each other as well. Just like you need to know the students' names, the other children want to know each other's names too.

Lastly, if all this fails you will have to go to plan B. Just keep in mind you cannot spend too much time with a shy student. The other students are in class to have fun too. They will soon become bored and will start playing around. Then you will have an even bigger problem.

So what is plan B? Plan B is to really be in communication with the parent. Parents are going to be disappointed if their child is shy. You will need to reassure the parent their child is okay. It is perfectly normal for a preschooler to be shy. If the child did not participate at all in the class, have the parent talk to their child at home to get the child's feedback. Did they like the class? Do they want to go back? Sometimes ballet is just not for them and they don't want to participate. If this is the case, they probably won't join the class. If they go home and tell Mom the class looked fun and they really do like to dance, it will just take some time before they start to trust you and join in.

Let me tell you about a student I had in the past:

Example:

Three year old Kristyna was extremely shy on the first day of class in September. She would not participate and would not leave Mom's side.

Mom told me how much she loved to dance therefore I was hopeful she would join in eventually. The next few classes Kristyna danced over in the corner where Mom was sitting. Sometimes Kristyna would come out into the middle of the room and dance with the rest of the class but would always go back to Mom. Mom then started to ease her way out of class little by little each week. She even took a magazine with her and read it to seem as if she was not paying attention to Kristyna. Finally, Mom was out of the classroom and by December Kristyna was running into class all by herself ready to tell me the latest news about her new ballerina necklace or ballet book. Mom was able to wait in the waiting area with the other parents. The process took a very long time but it was worth it! Kristyna took my classes all through her preschool years. I give the mom so much credit for being patient with her daughter. We all worked together to make the best experience for Kristyna.

Be patient with your shy dancers and the parents as well. If you all work together, you will have happy little dancers that trust you as their teacher.

Handling Different Ages in the Same Class

In my recreational pre-ballet classes I can have children ranging from age three (sometimes I will let a two year old in the class) through age six. How do you have a class with such different ages in the same class and keep everyone listening and happy?

Example #1:

A teacher is frustrated because a three year old in her class is not listening and the five and six year olds are bored because they are tired of the teacher constantly paying attention to the littler ones. What do you do?

You do not want to dwell on one child that doesn't listen and will need to act quickly in this situation. Remind everyone, in a fun, way they need to have their listening ears on and then with lots of fun energy move into whatever activity you are doing. Maybe you will have to grab the three year old's hand and dance with them. The important thing is not to stop for too long or you will lose the focus of the class.

Example #2:

You have two six year olds in your class that can't stop talking to each other. The younger students are having trouble paying attention to you because they are paying attention to the older girls.

In this case, remind the older students they are examples to the younger ones and need to be your helpers in class. Maybe they can help demonstrate steps or hold the younger one's hands. As a last resort, if necessary, tell the older girls if they can't stop talking while you are talking they will have to be separated. Give them a warning and then separate them for one song or activity if they keep it up.

The bottom line is, it is possible to have different ages in the same class. You just need to keep the class moving at all times. Give the older children a bit more technique if you would like to make the class more of a challenge for them. Don't stop for too long though. The little ones will have fun trying to keep up, but they are all still young and want to just move and have fun! At this point however, children in this age range all learn the same way, which is through creativity and big energy.

What to Do if Your Class Is Out of Control

There may be times when your class, for whatever reason, does get out of control. Maybe a parent had to speak with you during class or you had to pause to tie a bunch of your students' little ballet shoes. If you must stop your class, here are some tips to minimize the chaos and have your students back on track quickly.

If an adult has to speak to me in the middle of my class, I make sure the students are sitting down while I am talking. I may tell them they can pick an animal and sit quietly for a moment. I know they won't be completely quiet for that time period, but by giving them something quiet to do it will not be as difficult to bring them back into class when I am ready.

If I have to pay attention to one or more students because of tying little ballet shoes, I will talk to my students while I am tying the shoes. I will make jokes such as, "What am I, a shoe tier or a dance teacher?" To avoid spending too much time tying shoes I do remind the students not to intentionally untie their shoes. You will notice at times students will untie their shoes just to get your attention. Definitely talk to the parents about how to keep ballet shoe tied and tucked in so you won't have to deal with them at all.

When more than one or two students are occupied with something other than what they should be doing in your class it is the perfect time to play the "sit down, stand up" game I mentioned earlier. You can play with your class, have a great time and have everyone listening.

Keeping all of your students listening can be a challenge. By being a detective and figuring out quickly what the issue may be with a student, you can make sure to have a smoothly run class. Children do want to have fun, and if you are able to let them know your class is super fun you will have their attention.

Have Patience

When all is said and done remember to be patient with your students and with yourself. It does take time for small children to learn how to be in a class. If you stick to your rules and repeat them week after week your class will catch on. They will eventually know what you expect and what to do when they come into your classroom.

Patience with yourself is also important. If your class isn't running perfectly make sure to give yourself a break. It takes time for you to learn how to manage a class of preschoolers. You need to observe their behavior over time to understand them. You also need to allow yourself the freedom to try new things and see what works and what doesn't. There is a lot to be explored and learned. Even teachers who have been teaching for years have new things to learn all the time. They may learn about new ideas from other teachers they haven't thought of before. They may also become bored of activities they have used over the years and want to experiment with something new. Sometimes new ideas work out great and other times not so much. That is how we learn and grow.

Sometimes your class may have an extra tricky student that may feel beyond your reach. Although I never advocate giving up. There are always new ideas to try and you never know when something might work. Even though a student may be overwhelming don't give up. However we do need to recognize a student that is hard to manage and believe it is okay to give ourselves a break from time to time.

Take a deep breath, try your best and after class treat yourself to a message or a treat!

Chapter 5 "Pointes" to Remember

* Be One Step Ahead
* Know What is Fun
* Learn How to Tell if the Students Are Having Fun
* Have Designated Dance Spots
* Have Children Sit "Criss-Cross Apple Sauce"
* Teach Students to Raise Their Hands

* Use the Freeze Dance
* Keep the Class Positive
* Keep the Class Moving
* Don't Ask Yes or No Questions
* Give Warnings
* Let the Children Know Your Expectations
* Be a Detective
* Don't Be Afraid to QuestionYourself
* Help Shy Students
* Learn How to Handle Different Ages in the Same Class
* Learn What to Do if Your Class is Out of Control
* Have Patience

Chapter 6

Safety

S afety is so important when you are teaching a class for children. The class must be controlled in order for there to hopefully be no accidents. Preschool children have so much to learn about the world around them. You are responsible for them and need to make sure they stay safe at all times.

Safety in the Classroom

How do you keep your students safe while they are in your care? There are a few simple things you can do to make sure you have a safe class.

First, make sure the children are spread out in order for them to have room to move. You can easily do this by making spots on the floor for them to stand. We talked previously about many ways to make dancing spots for your students. Preschoolers will stand right next to their friend not understanding they might bump into each other. Having spots will help them spread out so they can dance freely.

Second, let the students know they must keep their hands to themselves. We don't want poking, pinching, hitting, kicking etc. in class. Even if their touch is gentle, other children may not want to be touched. Then you will have an upset child in class. The children can also become too excited when they start poking at each other and get distracted. It is best to have them keep their hands to themselves unless they are supposed to hold hands for an activity.

Third, I have a rule there is no running in class. Anything we can do to prevent children from hurting themselves is a must. There are plenty of other ways for the students to "run around". Have them chassé, skip, jump or leap around the space. Always make sure the students are moving around in the same direction. They can all move to the right or left, clockwise or counter clockwise, etc. This will help avoid collisions. It is a good idea to dance around with them when doing a high energy activity until the students become used to your style. When they can follow you they are more likely to move in the direction you are moving.

Lastly, when using props make sure you go over the rules about how to use the props with the children:

* Preschoolers still put things in their mouths. Let the children know the props do not go in their mouths.

* Props cannot be hit on anything. For example, shakers cannot be used to bang on walls, floors, or on other children.

* Scarves and parachutes can be very slippery when they are on a floor that has a hard, smooth surface like a dance floor. Make sure the children do not step on either a scarf or a parachute when they are on the floor because

they will slip and fall.

* Don't let children go on top of a parachute and under a parachute at the same time. Preschoolers don't pay attention to others around them and can easily bump into each other and hurt themselves.

There are rules the children need to follow. There should be no exception to these rules. This way, you can have fun dancing and playing with less worry. Always trust your gut if your are worried an activity is not controlled and needs to be stopped. Safety always comes first.

Going Out of the Classroom

You, as the teacher, are responsible for your class at all times. This is especially true if you have closed classes or if the parents drop their children off during class. How do you handle your class if you all need to travel outside of the dance room?

Let's use an example of when a child has to go to the bathroom and their parent is not there to take them. What should you do? Well, if one child has to go to the bathroom then the whole class needs to go to the bathroom. Remind parents to take their children to the bathroom before class has begun. Then, hopefully, you won't have to deal with bathroom trips very often. If you are lucky enough to have the bathroom in the same room in which you are teaching, then you can watch your students go in and out and keep your class going at the same time.

If the bathroom is outside the classroom, gather all the children in one line with you in front at the door. The students must follow you in a straight line down the hall to the bathroom. If your class is large, the students can find a buddy and hold hands two by two in a line. It is always helpful to play a game while you go down the hall as well. Can we pretend to be quiet, sneaky kitties while we walk down the hall? Can we walk on tip toe like ballet dancers?

Before leaving the room tell the students the teacher always opens the doors. Then they won't open the door and run through without you. Count your students often to make sure no one is left behind. You never know if a child found a fun plant or bug in the hall and has stopped to investigate.

While walking down the hall everyone must walk and talk quietly. If there are other classes going on in your building, the children should be respectful and quiet. When you arrive at the bathroom, everyone needs to go in the bathroom together if it is big enough. The children that do not have to go to the bathroom must stand with their backs against the walls and wait patiently. If the class looks antsy play a game such as "I Spy" or "Simon Says" while you wait for the other students.

You can safely venture out of the dance room with your class. The key is to keep everyone together, calm and paying attention to you with clear rules and fun games.

When Class is Over

How do you handle your class when the class is finished? Do your students just tear out of class wildly? Or can you play a fun game to have them safely exit the room? There are many options. Be creative in order for you continue to have a safe class even when it is over.

At the end of the class we don't want children to just run out of the room and find their parents. This is especially true if you teach at a location with a door leading to the outside or another part of a building. If a parent is late, you may not notice a child has run off to go look for them and when the parent comes, nobody knows where the child went.

If you are somewhere that has an outside area that is contained, you can let the children go into the hall or lobby, but make sure they know they have to stay with you until they see a parent. Watch your class closely to assure everyone does find Mom or Dad. Even if a parent or student would like to talk to you right after class politely tell them to wait a moment. This way you can watch your students until you know everyone is safely in the arms of someone they trust.

Again, if you let your students go out of the room to find their parents, don't let them run. Make up a fun game to play as they walk out of the room just like we talked about before when walking down the halls. Walk out like an animal or choose a fun ballet step as they go out of the dance studio. Whatever you have them do, ask them to do it quietly and have them follow you. Tell them, "Let's show your families how quiet we can be!" Make being quiet a game.

When I teach in a school or a larger building with other people and classes going on I think it is best to have the children sit criss-cross apple sauce in the room when class is over and have the parents come inside to pick them up. I always remember I am in charge of these precious little ones until they are with Mom or Dad. I tell the children to sit like a pretzel (However we are already sitting because I just had them sit to receive stamps at the end of class). Then I tell them to wait quietly until they see someone to pick them up inside the room. Finally, I let the parents in the room. Now I can easily see a family member come in and pick up each child. If someone is late, the child is still sitting with me and we can wait together. It is very simple and smooth. Parents also will see, when they come in, how controlled my class is because all the children are sitting and waiting quietly.

We don't want an accident after class. Having a controlled class when the class is over also strengthens the children's view of you as someone who is always in control no matter where you are or what you are doing. The parents will also see you are in control as well, and respect you even more as a teacher.

Safety is very important in a dance class. Children are dancing and moving all over the place and they should be. You need to be able to stay in control and enforce your rules at all times so no one is hurt or lost. Go back to the section about being one step ahead of the students and keeping the class fun. If you do this, the students will listen better and your chances for injuries will lessen.

Chapter 6 "Pointes" to Remember

* You Must Be Safe In the Classroom
* You Must Be Safe When Going Out of the Classroom
* You Must Be Safe When Class is Over

Chapter 7

Extras

T here are a few extra subjects I would like to talk about, including handling performances, working with parents and social media. In order for you to have the best class you can you must understand a few other components that go in to being a great teacher.

Dance Performances

A dance performance with preschoolers is just too cute for words! In their little tutus and sparkles they look like perfect Sugar Plum Fairies and Princes. How do you, as a teacher, make the experience a comfortable and memorable one for the students and parents?

First, where is your show going to be? Is this a big recital with a large studio? Or is it an informal presentation in the dance room? How you prepare your students may depend on the program at which you teach.

If you are teaching at a large studio, your students will probably work on their recital dances for at least a few months. At recital time they should know their dances pretty well. You will probably still need to dance with them however, because onstage they may become overwhelmed and forget what they are doing. They might forget where they stand, tug on their tutus or wave at their families. You will need to lead them enthusiastically to keep their focus.

In a more informal setting or a recreational program, you will probably not spend as much time on the final dances. Therefore, you will need to dance with the children the whole time just as big and enthusiastically as you would in class. You may even need to talk to the students like you were in a normal class. Just stand off to the side a bit so you are not in the way of the parents viewing.

Where ever your show is, make sure you talk to the children about the performance ahead of time. At a studio you can start talking to the students well in advance. In other settings, you can mention that families are going to be invited to watch a few weeks before.

Talk to the students about what exactly is going to happen. Let them know where they will be, and what will be expected of them. Go through what will happen on the stage and off and make it sound super exciting! Will they be backstage for a long time? Who will be with them? Will there be things to do? When will they see their moms and dads? Where will you be when they are on stage? You must let them know you will be there for them if they need to watch you at all times. Tell them they will never be left by themselves.

Example:

A four year old is all ready for her big recital. She is backstage with her costume on and will soon go on stage. Suddenly she has a realization, "I don't know my dances! What am I going to do on stage?" She didn't know her teacher would be dancing on stage with the class. She pretends she has to go to the bathroom and asks the teacher to find her parents. The child tells her parents she is too nervous to go on stage and wants to go home. Her parents agree to take her home and the child misses out on her recital.

(Yes, this was also me.)

Years later, and as a dance teacher, I wish someone would have told me my teacher was going to dance on the side of the stage in order for me to follow along if needed. I took class with my cousin, who was also four at the time, and to this day she teases I left her to dance on stage by herself! If there had been more communication I would have been fine.

It is perfectly natural for students to be nervous before a show. Reassure them you will be there with them every step of the way. I also tell the students, when we are nervous, it feels like we have butterflies flying around in our tummies and we just need to take slow, deep breaths to calm them down. Most of the time, the students will be fine and have a wonderful experience. Every now and then you will have a student who is just too shy to dance and wants to be with Mom or Dad and that's okay too!

Remember these are young children and whatever happens, happens. I have seen many interesting things from young students on stage over the years. Be ready to expect anything. Sometime shy students come out of their shells. Or the opposite happens. Students who were hams in class suddenly become very shy on stage. Some students who don't seem to pay attention in class will suddenly know all the steps. Some students won't dance at all, and some will act silly to get a laugh from the audience. You may even have a potty accident on stage! Expect the unexpected. Remember it is all normal.

Communicating to the parents about what to expect is also a necessity. Parents may be nervous leaving their child backstage. Reassure them you have everything under control and let them know what they can expect before the show. Unless the parent is a helper they shouldn't go backstage but rather into the audience and enjoy the show. If a parent is nervous they may make their child nervous as well. Separation is best in this situation.

Some parents of preschoolers also won't understand getting up on stage can be a bit unsettling. For some students getting up on stage is an exciting experience. For other students it can be scary. Parents need to know if their child isn't ready to perform that is okay. My mom jokingly complains she spent so much time putting my lion costume together, in the recital I mentioned above when I was four, and I didn't even dance. However my parents didn't make me feel bad about it. Parents all want their children to have fun and shine on stage. Just like a parent might feel upset their child is shy, they will also feel upset their child isn't performing. That something is wrong with them. Let the parents know these are young children and we can't always control how they are going to feel and what they are going to do. Let them know we can all try our best but we don't want to force a child to perform.

If you do have a child that is so nervous they might not perform there are a few things you can try. I first try to distract the student. Get them talking about other things. Talk about their beautiful costume. Ask who is in the audience to see them dance? Ask if they have any brothers, sisters or pets? Do they have a favorite character? If they calm down talking to you don't bring up their fear about performing. Hopefully they will settle in and feel better. If they are still very upset, mom or dad might have to come backstage and sit with them or you or the parent may have to go out and dance with them. If nothing works, don't push it. We want the students to remember dance is fun.

That is more important than pushing them on stage. Most of the time everyone has a fantastic time! This is the best time of the year. Our students have a chance to show off what they have learned and they are so proud of themselves. Always praise them no matter how they did. Even after all the years I have been teaching, performances with preschoolers are my absolute favorite. This is because the children are cute no matter what. Dancing or not dancing, tutus falling down, fingers in their noses and always adorable!

Closed Classes

You may, at one point or another, have to decide whether or not you would like to have open or closed classes. There are pluses and minuses for both. Decide for yourself, if it is up to you, what you think is best for your program and your students.

Closed classes are classes in which families or friends, are not allowed to observe class from inside the classroom. I know many teachers and studios battle with this issue. We teachers all know a class runs much smoother when the parents are out of the dance area. However, some teachers and studios worry parents will not sign their child up for class at a place that doesn't allow them to watch. Therefore they allow parents in the dance room in hopes of having more customers. If you are lucky and have the funds, your studio can have a one way mirror or even a window in your dance room. This way, parents can watch their children without being in the same room and interrupting your classes.

There are many reasons to have closed classes. First, the children really do listen better when there are no other distractions in the room. Children can act up around other people, especially their parents. If a child loves attention he or she will act like a clown when they have an audience. If, on the other hand a child is very shy, they may not even join the class if other people are watching. Or, a child might just want to hang out with Mom or Dad for any old reason. Children may run back and forth to their parents all through class as well. They might be hungry or thirsty or just want a hug. It is all very cute but as soon as one does it, they all want to do it and soon your class is just students running back and forth to their parents.

Another reason to have closed classes is because of the parents' behavior believe it or not. Parents, of course, are completely focused on their own children and have no idea what it takes to teach a class, let alone a class of preschoolers. Your attention is already spread pretty thin. You have to watch the children and make sure they are learning, having fun, behaving and being safe while remembering your curriculum and teaching it in an exciting way! When you have Mom sitting on the sidelines telling Susie to point her toes it is much more difficult. Parents will tell their children what to do, they will talk with the other parents or talk on their phones and they will let little brother or sister wander through your class and think it is adorable. Then it is up to you to tell them to be quiet or to please take their child out of the dance space. I feel this is an unnecessary job for an instructor. You should only have to teach the children, not manage the parents.

Lastly, because there are not any outside disruptions in a closed class, you can actually accomplish more in your classes. The students will be able to perform more dances and play more games. You can also teach more elaborate steps to the children. At the preschool level we are not talking about fouettés or anything like that, but you will have better concentration from the students to try more challenging preschool appropriate steps and choreography.

Closed classes are beneficial for you and your students. You, as a dance teacher, are free to teach your class without any outside interruptions. You can be more relaxed to teach what you want instead of having to mold your class to any limitations.

I feel I cannot teach the way I am meant to when I have to deal with anything other than my students. I have a responsibility to teach the best class I can, and I can only do when I have closed classes.

However, I am not as strict about having closed classes today as I once was. I try my best to keep the parents out of the dance room but I will leave the door open so they can watch if they would like. I am also lucky to have a couple spaces where there are windows for parents to view classes.

As the years have passed I feel parents are also becoming more and more anxious about leaving their child with someone they don't know. That makes the case for having closed classes more challenging. Closed classes can help us run the best class we can but the concerns of parents do need to be addressed. If they feel nervous try your best to reassure them about their fears. You may need to have more designated observation times during your class sessions.

"Observation Days" are great for both parents and students. If you have closed classes be sure to invite the parents into the class every once in a while for a special viewing. If you have short sessions these can be on the last day of class. You can decide if you are going to let the parents watch the whole class or just the last bit of class. I let parents watch the last 15 minutes of class because preschool students do not have much of an attention span. I have tried longer than this but lost the students and the audience (little brothers and sisters) before the class was finished. The children will be overwhelmed when they see mom, dad, grandma and grandpa with cameras. Keep it short and sweet.

If you are not in charge of the program at which you are teaching, whether or not parents are allowed in the room with their children will already be decided for you. If parents are in the room you will have to do your best. Let's talk about what to do if you have parents in your dance space.

If you work at a location where parents are allowed in the dance room, here are some tips for dealing with this situation. Parents and students will all need to know your rules and when they don't follow them, you will have to give reminders.

Here are a few examples you will have to consider:

* Do you want the students to come to you when they need their shoes tied or can they go to Mom?
* Can they leave if they want a drink of water?
* Can parents parent from the sidelines or do you want to be in charge of discipline?
* When the parents start talking to each other too loudly you will have to nicely ask them to quiet down.
* When Susie's little brother wants to join class you will have to take him back to Mom if Mom doesn't come grab him.

Remember, however, never be upset or rude when dealing with the parents. These are your customers. Give reminders in a polite and friendly way.

Being a parent, I completely understand the want and need for parents to watch their children in a class. I love to watch my kids! Not only is it fun but I, just like any parent, want to make sure my children are safe and behaving in class. I may also want to check up on the teacher and make sure my child is learning. However as a teacher I know how dance classes run with and without an audience. There is a definite difference.

Classes can be held with parents watching and students can learn, it is just not as effective in my opinion. You, as a teacher, can try different ways to see what you prefer. If you have the choice, you can make your own decision as to whether or not parents will watch your classes.

Issues With Parents

If you have a parent that has an issue with you, your teaching or the program at which you teach, you need to know how to handle it in a professional manner. If you are working for someone else's program, you will first need to talk to your program director asap. They will want to put an end to any conflict quickly to satisfy their customers. If your program director is not available at the time, you will need to deal with the situation yourself and go to them at a later time.

First of all, if a parent has a complaint, make sure you listen calmly. Don't talk back and become defensive. Just listen. Second, if you are in charge, try to come up with a solution to the parent's complaint if possible. If you are not in charge, tell the parent you will let your program director know immediately and they will contact them with a solution soon. Finally, follow up with the parent after a solution is made to see if they are satisfied.

Here is an example of a situation a teacher of mine was in recently with an upset parent and how she handled it like a pro:

Example:

I run my classes through community programs. Therefore, there are three different entities that deal with the parents of my students; the community center, my instructor and myself. We all need to make sure we have good communication with the parents. One location I offer classes with sends out email confirmations to the parents when the parent signs their children up for an activity. For one particular camp, a parent was upset because she did not receive an email confirmation her registration went through and her children were all set for class. When they arrived to the class, the mom let my instructor know she was unhappy. My instructor was great. She apologized even though she had nothing to do with the email process. She told the parent to talk to the community center's office to ask why they had not sent her an email and she would mention the parent's complaint to me. Because the instructor handled the situation so well by being calm and listening to the parent, the parent actually felt satisfied right away and never even talked to the community center or myself. I went to the class on the last day and spoke with the mom and she was completely over the whole situation. My instructor was able to calm her down to the point she let it go completely. Problem solved!

We first need to listen calmly to any complaint. Then try not to become defensive. Talk out the issue with the parent and your supervisor to find a solution to the problem. When a solution is found, let the parent know.

Sometimes a solution can't be found and you just have to do your best to keep your happy face on and hope the parent understands. A parent may have an issue with a policy you have that you are not willing to change. You may lose a customer and that sometimes happens. Remember you can't please all the people all the time and that is okay.

I believe teaching is a gift, and as teachers we are rewarded by the wonderful gifts our students share with us. However, students can challenge us and their parents can as well. Dance teachers are in a business that needs customers to survive. In my experience, it does not do any good to confront a parent even if you are not at fault. Just listen and try your best to satisfy your customers. We will all run into parents and students who are upset for one reason or another. We need to rise above the negativity, take a deep breath and let it go with a smile on our face. In the end, everyone will be happier.

Selling Your Class

I would like to touch a bit on how to sell your class. Even if you are not the studio owner for the class where you are teaching, you are still selling your class. In every job we have, we are selling a product or service to customers.

If you teach a class for a program, and the next session your students don't return, the owner of that program is going to question your teaching and may look for someone else to take your place. You want to not only keep your students, but hopefully build your classes by word of mouth.

Therefore, how do you sell your class? There are a few things you will need to consider: 1) You need to price the class appropriately 2) offer the classes in a convenient location and 3) have a high quality class. If you are not the studio owner, the price of the class or the location of the studio will be out of your control. I will talk however, as if you are in control of all the factors.

How should you price your classes? You need to take a look at where you offer your classes. Are you in a more affluent suburb or a working class community? What are other similar programs charging? What is the economy like? Are people doing well or having a hard time making ends meet? What is your overhead? How much do you need to charge in order to stay in business? What do you want as take home pay at the end of the day? All of these factors must be considered. The easiest way to set a price is to take a look at similar programs in your area and try to be competitive. This means, charge close to what they are charging or less if you can afford to do so. However don't sell yourself short and charge too little either. People may think you are not very good if you don't charge enough. Also if you charge too little you may not be able to afford to stay in business. Make sure you have a good business plan in order for you to know exactly what your expenses are. If you can, talk to parents in your area to find out what they are willing to pay. Getting as much feedback as you can before you begin is always a great idea.

Where should you locate your business? Try to go where you see there is a need for classes. It is very hard to compete in a location with many dance studios. Go out into the outer suburbs of your community if you have to. Offering different types of classes can work as well. If there are many large competitive studios in your area, start with something smaller and more recreational. Again, see if you can talk to parents to find out what they are looking for.

As far as how to have a high quality class, follow all of the points I have made in this guidebook to teach the best class you can. If you do that, you will be selling your classes. Here is a review of the main points:

* Be Enthusiastic Around Your Parents and Students
* Genuinely Care About Your Students
* Be Passionate About Teaching
* Be Well Organized
* Look Neat and Clean
* Have Big Energy
* Control Your Class in a Positive Way
* Know Your Material
* Have Fun!

Remember you are not only selling your classes but you are selling yourself. If your students and the parents of your students like you, they will be more likely to sign up again and again!

Diversity

Every meeting I have with new instructors who come to work for my program, I make sure I touch on the subject of diversity. We are in a time of inclusion for all. Everyone shouldn't be put in the same box. Dance typically has been a place of sameness. Same costumes, same hairstyles, same kicks and turns etc. In my program I am not concerned that all my students kick the same height or their appearance is the same. I want to attract children from all different backgrounds and abilities. Therefore what I do need to be concerned with is that all my students feel welcome, learn and have fun. When we talk about diversity what exactly are we talking about? As dancers we can first talk about being inclusive to people with different body types, however we need to go further than that. We also need to take into consideration gender, race and ability.

I make a point to let my students know our bodies are not all the same and that is okay. I am a great example of someone that loves dancing ballet but doesn't necessarily have what others might think are the right feet or the best turn out, etc. In my school that is okay. There needs to be a place, where students who don't fit in to the typical mold of what people think a dancer should be, can go to dance. Dance is a wonderful art that should be able to be expressed by anyone who wishes to do so. Not only is dance wonderful to express but the benefits of dance are endless for people of all ages. Why would we deprive anyone of that opportunity?

Gender equality is another factor that needs to be considered in your classes. Dance classes seem to consist of mostly girls. Is your class curriculum suitable for boys? Will boys feel welcome? It is easy for a preschool ballet classes to be all about princesses, fairies and unicorns. Make sure there are a few princes or other male or gender neutral characters in your activities in order for boys to feel included. Some children may also not fit into typical gender stereotypes. Be aware of the needs of all your students in order for everyone to have fun!

Are your classes inclusive to all ethnicities and races? We don't all have the same traditions and backgrounds. We need to make sure a child doesn't feel left out or shamed for their family's beliefs. It is also wonderful that costumes, tights and ballet shoes now come in different skin tones for students of different colors. It is hard to believe it has taken so long for that to be the case. Not all of us have the same skin tones. Dancewear should reflect that.

Dance classes may also have children with disabilities. Extra care needs to be given to include a child that may not be able to handle the material the same way as other children. I have had children with autism, down syndrome or other physical disabilities in my dance classes. It does take some extra planning when a child with a disability is in your class. They might need a bit of extra attention or need the choreography altered a bit. If you put the extra effort into the process it works out just fine and is a rewarding experience for everyone.

Our world is becoming more and more aware of the needs of each individual in our society. We always hear about how far we have to go and it is true. There is more work to be done to make sure everyone feels included, respected and safe. However we do need to celebrate where we are. We are talking more about the subject and educating each other every day. Anyone should be allowed to be who they are meant to be especially in the wonderful world of dance!

Our Online World

The internet is an amazing resource for dance teachers. It can provide us with information about anything we want to know in the dance world. We can learn about dance history, technique, companies and schools. We can connect with other dancers and dance teachers and ask for advice and share stories. We can look for opportunities to continue our studies or find performing and teaching jobs. There is an abundance of information.

The internet has been extremely beneficial in my teaching career. If I am searching for song choices, creative movement activities or recital ideas there are always places to go and find this information. There are so many positive reasons to use the internet today if you are a dancer. However there can be a downside. We must make good choices in order to get the most out of this resource and be supportive to our fellow artists.

The downside to the internet is sometimes people forget to be respectful when commenting online. It takes courage to ask a question, share a story or post a performance on social media.

Posting a negative comment does not benefit anyone in any way. It is hurtful to the person sharing, to the many people reading it and also to the person making the negative statement. Spreading negativity is never the right choice. It just spreads more negativity. If you don't agree with something my advice is just to let it go. It might be one person's opinion and not something to worry about. If you feel strongly about speaking out do it with compassion and understanding. Otherwise there is no need to ever make a negative comment. Choose to be supportive!

Luckily what I have loved the most about the dance teaching world online are the wonderful communities I have found on social media and message boards. People are so supportive to each other. Teachers are asking for and giving advice in positive ways. There are questions asked about running a class or dance studio, tips for teaching technique, song ideas, etc. and so many people are willing to respond and help out. The passion in the world of dance teaching has inspired me immensely. So many of you put everything you have into passing the art of dance on to your students and will do anything to keep teaching. It is easy to see how important it is and how much love there is for this important art.

Another point to mention about being online is always be aware of your online presence when you are applying for a job. Whenever someone applies for a teaching position with my program I always search for them online. There have been people I have not hired because of what I have found on google or on their social media pages. We are in a business that works with children. It is important I hire people who I know will treat them well and keep them safe. Is there anything I can find online that will give me more of an idea of how they might interact with a class? I know a person's personal life may not reflect how they are professionally but it may have an impact. You need to be aware that what you put on social media can be a reflection of who you are. Are you representing yourself in a way that will be beneficial to your future? Is it in line with your goals? Mindfulness is key in this situation.

Not only should we be aware of how we are perceived through our social media but we can actually use the internet to promote ourselves. Many performers use social media to promote themselves as teachers and performers. They may also have a website including their bio, resume, videos of performances, etc. If someone is looking to hire you, having a website that points out all your positives will definitely help you get the job!

The internet is a wonderful tool. Use it to improve yourself as a dancer, instructor and a person and you will be on your way to success!

Chapter 7 "Pointes" to Remember

*   Handle Performances with Care
*   Closed Classes Can Be Beneficial
*   Handle Issues With Parents Respecfully
*   Sell Your Classes Effectively
*   Be Inclusive
*   Use Online Tools Responsibly

Conclusion

A while ago someone in my family, who lives out of town, was telling me about her four year old's ballet and tap class. Her daughter liked the class but the mom mentioned how so many of the children in the class didn't listen. Her four year old actually told the other children to listen to the teacher! It was funny because at the time I was in the middle of writing my first draft of this book on this very subject. I asked her what the teacher did about it. The mom said the teacher did not know how to control the class and it was her first year of teaching. "Of course." I thought. "That teacher needs to read my book!" There shouldn't be any reason a child in a class should have to tell the other children to listen. Fortunately there are plenty of tools now to help us all!

Parents of my students are always surprised to see how well my classes are run and I receive many positive comments. They cannot believe how well a group of preschoolers will listen, follow me and have fun. The secrets are all in this guidebook. You can achieve the same accolades if you work hard!

If you follow what I have outlined:

* You will be professional,
* You will have a fun class,
* You will have a safe class,
* Your class will listen and learn,
* You will be selling yourself well and
* You will be a great teacher!

Teaching preschool ballet is both fun and challenging. It is a great business to be in. Preschoolers love to move, explore and be creative. Your job is to channel that wonderful, positive energy into a class that lets your students be preschoolers and learn in a fun and safe way. What I have outlined, and hopefully what you now have a good grasp of, is how to keep the children following you while keeping the class fun at the same time. This is the trick. Actually, I have given you many "tricks" in order for you to accomplish your goals. These are ideas such as being happy to see everyone, knowing your material, having the students sit "criss-cross apple sauce" between activities, and so on. If applied, you will have a great class.

When I began writing this book, I didn't realize how much information I actually had to share. I thought this would be a small booklet for both new and experienced teachers to share ideas for running a great class. We teachers always need a fresh perspective and new ideas for our classes from time to time. As I was writing, I kept thinking about more and more ideas that needed to be included. Pretty soon I really had written a book!

However, I shouldn't have been surprised. Teaching is a complex art. Like I mentioned in the introduction, teaching can be a challenge, especially when you start out. First, you need to know the subject you are teaching. Second, you need to learn how to read your students and speak their language. Finally, you need to know how to pass your knowledge on to your students in order for them to actually learn how to dance ballet.

Most pre-ballet teachers and most dance teachers in general do not go to school to learn how to teach dance. We don't even need a degree to teach and most dance teachers at private dance studios don't have teaching degrees. If a teacher does have a dance education degree they usually go into the schools to teach. However, everyone still has to learn through experience and from the advice of teachers that have been there before.

Therefore, it is the responsibility of each individual teacher to get more training on his or her own. When I started teaching, I was fortunate to work with many wonderful teachers who taught me a great deal. The rest I learned from watching other teachers and through my own experiences. However, I never stop learning. I continue to take dance classes for my own growth, and perform when I have a chance. I also watch other teachers and read message boards when I can. I never think I am finished learning and growing as a teacher or dancer. I know I will be even better as the years go on. That is exciting! I can't wait to pass new ideas and activities on to my students!

Thank you for taking the time to do a service to yourself and your current and future dance students! Keep learning and growing and of course, keep dancing!

About the Author

Gina Mayer, aka "Ms. Gina Ballerina", is a teacher of all forms of dance and theater and has been teaching since 1996. Dance has always been a part of her life. It all started at age two when she told her mom she wanted to take dance classes and she never looked back.

Having a love for all forms of the performing arts led Gina to pursue tap, jazz, hip hop, ballet, voice and acting while growing up. She then went on to receive her BFA in theater and a minor in dance from the University of Minnesota in Duluth. Since graduating, she has had the privilege of performing with some great companies including the Guthrie Theater, the Chanhassen Dinner Theater and the Lyric Opera of NY.

In 2001 Gina and her husband moved to New York City. There, they had the opportunity to study with great voice and dance teachers, perform and teach. Gina loved the opportunities which included being the resident choreographer for the Pied Piper Children's Theater Company. It was while she was teaching in New York, Gina started to develop her *Wish Upon a Ballet*™ program for preschoolers. When she and her husband decided to start a family however, they moved back to Minnesota to be closer to home.

Since being back in Minnesota, Gina continues teaching dance and theater through her own program, Mayer Arts. Her classes are through community education and parks and recreation programs and are for families looking for something recreational, relaxed and affordable without sacrificing proper technique.

Gina continues to study dance and voice and believes artists are never finished perfecting their craft. She is fortunate to still take class and perform when she is not spending time teaching and being with her amazing family.

Connect With Me:

If you are in the Minneapolis/St. Paul area and are interested in my classes in dance and theater please visit www.mayerarts.com.

My free website all about ballet is, www.wish-upon-a-ballet.com. There, you can learn about everything ballet including more teaching tips, ballet history, ballet companies, famous ballet dancers and even a video dictionary of ballet terms.

Websites
mayerarts.com
wish-upon-a-ballet.com

Facebook: @WishUponABallet

Twitter: @WishBallet

Instagram: @wishuponaballet

Youtube: youtube.com/c/wuaballet

Other Books by Gina Mayer Available on Amazon -
How to Teach Preschool Ballet: A Guidebook for Teachers Ebook
Creative Movement Games for Preschool Ballet: Incorating Props Ebook